DRY HUMOR

TALES OF ARIZONA WEATHER

By JAMES E. COOK

Illustrated by JACK GRAHAM

Gem Guides Book Company
315 Cloverleaf Drive, Suite F
Baldwin Park, California 91706

Dry Humor: Tales of Arizona Weather
Copyright©1992 by Gem Guides Book Co.

Library of Congress Catalogue Card Number 92-52500
ISBN 0-935182-54-3

Published in the United States of America

Dedication

This book is for my mother, Ruby Cook, who helped me weather the storms of my life.

ACKNOWLEDGEMENTS

Without the help of veteran weather observer and wry philosopher Robert J. Schmidli, this would have been only a thin joke book. One of Schmidli's colleagues has nicknamed him, with fondness and respect, "Mr. Climate."

Bob retired from the National Weather Service in 1983, after 43 years of service. Eight years later, he was still volunteering several hours a day updating Arizona weather data. In addition to providing current statistics, he provided several background works, including his own *Climate of Arizona*, published by the National Weather Service; *Arizona Climate 1885-1895* and *Arizona Climate 1931-1972*, both published by the University of Arizona.

Sometimes facts are inadequate to describe Arizona weather. I coined some of the embellishments in this book, but most windies are ancient and untraceable. My friend Don Dedera corraled many veterans, including some of his and mine, in *The Cactus Sandwich and Other Tall Tales of the Southwest* (Northland Press, 1986). Some of its yarns served as templates for the refurbished folklore herein. Dedera granted permission to quote from the latest product of his own publishing house, Prickly Pear Press, *You Know You're An Arizona Native. . .*

Another loyal friend, Francis D. Nutt, spent 30 years gathering and publishing the landmark book *An Arizona Alibi*, the complete works of Dick Wick Hall. The world is indebted to her.

Thanks to historian Marshall Trimble, a skilled fabricator of what I call "truth-by-products," and to journalist and historian Rosalee Crowe, who has a fine sense of Yuma--her family's hometown for generations.

Most of the newspaper stories quoted here appeared originally in *The Arizona Republic* of Phoenix, founded in 1890 as *The Arizona Republican*. Some material appeared in recent columns and feature stories that I wrote for *The Republic*, my employer for 30 years. Special thanks to readers whose column contributions add spice to this book.

TABLE OF CONTENTS

CHAPTER 1

THE CURSE OF THE GILA MONSTER

In the summer of 1897, a Phoenix businessman decided to market the beaded, poisonous lizard called a Gila monster. He figured he could sell them to easterners, and to a growing number of tourists visiting Arizona.

He asked a Pima Indian to supply him with Gila monsters. The Pima recoiled. Did the white man not know that if a Pima touched a Gila monster in summer, the day would become unbearably hot, the temperature rising beyond the imagination of man?

Ninety-three years later, on June 26, 1990, it seemed as though a Pima had carelessly fondled a Gila monster. The temperature rose to 120 degrees on June 25, exceeding by 2 degrees the previous all-time record for Phoenix. On June 26, at 1:27 p.m., the temperature reached 121. At 2:47, as masochists stood by their radios, the temperature hit 122.

Patio furniture stood on one leg.

Sundials, which normally run 30 minutes fast in Arizona in summer, gained an entire time zone.

Hot air balloons turned inside out.

M&M candies, whose manufacturers boast that they melt in the mouth but not in the hand, were staining tiny fingers all over town.

The high temperature was recorded at Phoenix Sky Harbor International Airport, one of the hottest places in the Salt River Valley. But four other Arizona stations, including the nearby retirement community of Youngtown, also reported 122 degrees that afternoon. The 122 at Yuma was one degree short of an all-time high for that city. Tucson, usually five or six degrees cooler than Phoenix and Yuma, had a new record high of 117.

My co-worker Bonnie Baker has observed, "Whatever the weather does, people always say it has never done that here before." For once, they were right.

As a journalist, I was delighted to observe a truly original story. Yet I felt an edge of panic. What if the temperature did not stop rising, but continued upward to the point of incineration? Stepping outside, I felt like a gingerbread boy being popped into the witch's oven.

My life flashed before my eyes. I realized I had spent 28 per cent of that life enduring desert summers.

Graham

Another 10 per cent was spent fighting bitter winter cold in Arizona's high mountains. It was time to write the book that blows the lid off Arizona's weather.

Weather is the first topic of conversation in Arizona, whether you're a winter visitor savoring the balmy days of January, a new resident enduring your first summer, or a jaded native.

Florida calls itself "The Sunshine State," but in Miami the sun shines only 73 percent of the time alloted for daylight. The percentage of possible sunshine is 86 in Phoenix and Tucson, 91 in Yuma. Sunshine has been the making of southern Arizona cities, creating jobs and attracting new residents and tourists from anyplace that has icy winters.

However, the sunshine statistic becomes a dubious distinction in July. On the deserts of southern and western Arizona, summer heat is formidable, legendary, sometimes preposterous. Arizona is one of the few places that does not switch to daylight savings time in summer. It already has enough daylight to export some, and saving more would create a storage problem.

During the 1990 heat wave, Arizona made the evening news on at least four networks. Turner Broadcasting Company's Weather Channel dispatched a reporter from Atlanta just to cover the hot spell.

It had been hotter in Arizona. The temperature reached 127 at Fort Mohave in 1896, and again at Parker in 1905. During the decade of the 1980s, Bullhead City in northwestern Arizona reported the nation's highest temperature more days that any other reporting station.

But never had it been hotter in the Phoenix metropolitan area, where more than half the state's population lives. Tourism promoters sometimes use "mean temperature" to downplay the heat, advertising the midpoint between average daily highs and lows to suggest that summer heat is not so harsh as people think. The temperature was never meaner than it was in June, 1990.

Resort owners had been conducting a fresh "Summer's No Sweat" campaign to convince potential visitors that the summer heat need not be debilitating. They fell strangely silent after Phoenix made the world news on June 26. Their billboards faded in the sun.

Airlines cancelled some flights from Phoenix Sky Harbor on June 26, fearing that some airplanes might not be able to take off. Technical manuals vouched for their behavior only to 120 degrees. Had the mythical Greek Icarius tried his wings of feathers and wax on such a day, he wouldn't have left the hangar.

Several entrepreneurs, spiritual successors to the would-be vendor of Gila monsters, flooded the market with T-shirts testifying that the wearer had survived a day of 122-degree heat in Phoenix, Arizona, USA.

People around the world also seem to know that while the East and the Midwest suffer a suffocating, humid heat, Arizona enjoys "a dry heat," which makes the temperature seem not nearly so hot. This happens to be true.

In the summer of 1990, however, it became apparent that what Arizona offers most is a *hot* heat.

But Arizona's lively weather offers more than mere high temperatures. Within weeks of the June 26 landmark, Phoenix made the national news again (and later the television show *Emergency 911*), as flash floods threatened the lives of careless motorists. And by year's end, snow hit the city--not the freaky trace that arrives in the desert city once every few years, but 24 hours of intermittent flurries.

Around Christmas, a record cold snap broke water pipes all over the Phoenix area and froze millions of tender, semi-tropical plants beyond recovery. Heavy snow and sub-zero temperatures brought human activity to a halt in the state's mountain regions.

Even native Arizonans don't think of theirs as a "mountain state," but it has a lot of them. Ironed out flat, the state might be larger than Texas. One winter it snowed 400.9 inches in the White Mountains of eastern Arizona.

Describing Arizona's climate is a bit more complex than describing the climate of, say, Connecticut. At 113,956 square miles, Arizona is the sixth-largest state in the nation, larger than several eastern states combined. Elevations range from about 75 feet above sea level to 12,643 feet, covering six "life zones," including the bottom few feet of the zone labeled "arctic-alpine."

Southern and western regions of Arizona are part of the Sonoran desert, lowest and hottest of North American deserts. The northeastern part of the state is a vast, semi-arid plateau region. The two areas are separated by a diagonal region of mountains that make New Hampshire seem like a theme park. And southern Arizona has several abrupt, isolated ranges rising from the desert floor, where mountains should not logically be. Chauvinistic Arizonans note that these "sky islands" are taller than anything in the eastern part of the country.

A couple of times, there has been an 89-degree spread between temperatures within Arizona. On October 16, 1973, the morning low was 16 at Alpine in the White Mountains; the afternoon high was 105 at Gila Bend on the Sonoran desert. In 1989 and 1990, Arizona was one of a handful states from which both the nation's high and low temperatures were reported at one time or another (but never on the same day).

Back to 1990: Less than nine months after the record hot spell, a near-record March storm dumped more than 30 inches of snow in the high country, and several inches of rain on the deserts, rescuing the state overnight from drought.

The Search for Seasons

Much of our weather lore is pinned on mythical ranchers and grizzled desert rats, but Arizona is one of the most urbanized states in the nation. Three-fourths of the population lives in the Phoenix and Tucson metropolitan areas. These urbanites, like their almanac-reading neighbors in the outback, talk mostly about the weather.

Two-thirds of the people who live in Arizona came here from somewhere else, partly because they didn't want to shovel snow any more. And yet their most frequent complaint is that their new home lacks the four well-defined seasons found in other climates. But you can always find a season somewhere in Arizona. An editorial in a Phoenix newspaper January 3, 1897, told it better than I can:

"The sound of sleigh bells was heard in Prescott [5,354 feet] on New Year's Day, and cutters were seen flying about the town. The sun shone brightly on the snow. One hundred miles away, in the Salt River Valley, the sun was shining on green alfalfa shoots, flowers were blooming in the open and the sky was full of balm. In Arizona, if you do not find in one spot the kind of climate you want, a few hours' travel will bring the desired brand."

Nowadays, of course, it's easier to travel to another season. Phoenix residents regularly drive 150 miles to watch aspen leaves turn in the forests of northern Arizona.

It seems to me that if the Phoenix and Tucson areas are missing a season, it must be autumn. We have a decided winter, with hard frosts, but it lasts only a couple of months. When the groundhog steps outside on February 2, he's wearing sun block.

Spring is long and beautiful, if you don't expect a lot of April showers. Summer is longer, and harsh. Summer heat lasts until nearly Halloween. Then comes a kind of Indian summer; we often eat Thanksgiving dinner outdoors.

If autumn falls on a Sunday, it is observed the following Monday; then we are into winter. One year a young couple from New York state rented the house next door to ours. Being a trained observer, I noticed that the woman wore a bikini in her backyard well into December, when the rest of us were beginning to complain about the cold. By the following year, she had become acclimated and dressed like everyone else.

For contrast, there is Flagstaff, the hub of northern Arizona. It sits at 6,894 feet, and still enjoys 79 percent of possible sunshine. But during one freakishly cool summer, National Weather Service meteorologist Paul Sorenson threatened to plant his garden in a wheelbarrow so he could bring it into the house at night.

CONTRASTING CLIMATES

The lowest inhabited place in Arizona is Gadsden, south of Yuma. It is 95 feet above sea level, and hotter than 99-cent brake pads.

But there are two communities at 8,000 feet elevation: Alpine in the White Mountains of eastern Arizona, and Summerhaven in the Santa Catalina Mountains near Tucson.

Once, in an Idaho mountain town, the locals told the author that the latest frost on record there was June 30 and the earliest frost on record was July 1. Good joke, eh?

But not so far-fetched. In Alpine, the last frost comes around June 21 and the first around August 23. In Phoenix (1,100 feet elevation) the average dates are February 7 and December 13.

Or consider the Grand Canyon. Grand Canyon Village on the South Rim is at 6,826 feet and North Rim Lodge is at 8,200 feet, wintery elevations. However, Phantom Ranch at the bottom of the Canyon is at 2,500 feet. Because the canyon traps heat, the climate there is like that at Yuma, or Gadsden.

"You don't like our weather?" a Flagstaff resident says in spring. "Stick around fifteen minutes and it'll change."

I was born in Phoenix just before evaporative coolers became common. My parents concluded that I could not stand the summers, so we began a gypsy life, going north in summers to Arizona's mountains, where my father held a seasonal job with the U.S. Forest Service. He had found a low-budget way to do what residents of the Salt River Valley had always done: flee in summer.

We eventually quit Phoenix all together and I lived in several mountain places, including ten years in Flagstaff. I returned to live full-time in Phoenix when I was 27, and found that my parents had been correct: I could not stand desert summers. By that time, everyone had evaporative coolers, and many people had refrigerated air conditioning.

How did Arizonans survive before mechanical cooling? With great ingenuity, and considerable resignation. This book will tell you factually, about some of the scandalous behavior that resulted.

The Official History of Arizona Weather

Between about 1200 A.D. and the mid-1400s, several prehistoric civilizations "vanished" from Arizona. That is to say archaeologists could no longer trace their movements--some probably evolved into today's Native Americans, and some may have moved to San Diego.

The vanished people included the Sinagua (Spanish for "without water") and the Anasazi in the north, the Hohokam in the south. The latter people had built an elaborate system of irrigation canals which early Anglo settlers copied to turn the Salt River Valley into an agricultural empire, with several growing seasons.

Most scientists conclude that drought had something to do with the end of the earlier cultures. The ancients left some weather reports on the petroglyphs they etched on rocks throughout the territory, but most suggest thunderstorms and floods; "drought" was hard to draw.

Spanish explorers entered Arizona in 1539. They said the climate was already in place, and they would not be blamed for it. Father Juan Nentvig, a Jesuit priest, in 1764 inventoried that part of New Spain which included the future Arizona. He wrote, "The climate of Sonora is hot rather than temperate. . ." he also noted that the climate seemed to be healthy for the Indians who lived along the Colorado and Gila rivers.

As the United States took possession of the territory, observers from the U.,S. Corps of Topographical Engineers accompanied early expeditions, making notes on climate. Lt. Col. William Emory, who accompanied Col. Stephen Watts Kearney's Army of the West across Arizona in 1846, during the Mexican War, may have been the first to note the low humidity and how it effected temperature.

The first official U.S. Government weather observation was taken at Fort Defiance December 1, 1851, while the region was still part of New Mexico territory. Post Surgeon Dr. D.L. Magruder reported a high of 40 degrees Fahrenheit, a low of 12 degrees and occasional flurries of snow.

The weather was considerably balmier at Fort Mohave, where record-keeping began in 1859, and at Fort Yuma, where the records go back to 1870. (Fort Yuma was in California, but Army operations straddled the Colorado River.)

The National Weather Service (NWS) has five full-time, "first line" stations in Arizona: Phoenix, Tucson, Yuma, Flagstaff, Winslow. And there are nearly 300 "cooperative" weather stations, where observers report data to the NWS.

A flash flood in December, 1910, washed away the weather instruments in the Havasupai Indian village of Supai, deep in Havasu Canyon, an offshoot of the Grand Canyon. Weather observer Charles E. Coe barely escaped drowning.

Coe reported that many Havasupai people had been saved by one of their traditional beliefs: that they should head for higher ground around December 15. But traditions, like forecasts tend to be inexact. In September 1990 the latest of an untold number of floods swept through Supai, forcing the evacuation of 100 people.

Which brings us to a note of caution: This book makes light of Arizona's weather extremes, but we don't want anyone to die laughing. Many people have perished because of desert heat, mountain blizzards and flash floods. Traveling in Arizona in the extreme season requires planning, common sense and caution. Take it easy.

CHAPTER 2

THE TRAGIC DEMISE OF THE SAND TROUT

Before the Colorado River was dammed in seven places, it changed channels more often than a faulty television set, causing an occasional territorial dispute between Arizona and California.

A visiting journalist wrote in 1864, "A more capricious river does not exist. The main channel shifts so often that the most skillful (steamboat) pilot always knows where it is not to be found by pursuing the course of his last trip."

Years later, an Arizonan who lived on the bank of the river went out one morning to inspect the damage from an overnight flood. He found the river had cut a new channel around the other side of his house.

He went indoors and told his wife, "Well, we live in California now."

"Oh, thank God," she said. "I couldn't stand another summer in Arizona."

That's one of the older stories about Arizona heat, but not the oldest. One story is so tired that one hundred years ago, former Army officer John G. Bourke apologized profusely for including it in *On The Border With Crook*. And now, like Bourke, I dare not leave it out, for fear someone will think I have not heard the story.

It is about the soldier from Yuma who died and went to Hell. He soon sent back to Yuma for his blankets, because Hell was chilly by comparison.

That's it. That's the whole gag.

Here's what Bourke had to say about life in those frontier garrisons in the 1870s: "The heat in most of them became simply unendurable, although here the great dryness of the atmosphere proved a benefit. Had the air been humid, very few of our garrison would now be alive to tell of temperatures of one hundred twenty and over, and of days during the whole twenty-four hours of which the thermometer did not register below the one hundred notch.

"There was a story current that the heat had one time become so excessive that two thermometers had to be strapped together to let the mercury have room to climb."

J. Ross Browne, the magazine journalist who described the capricious Colorado in 1864, noted that the pleasant winter climate in the region surpassed that of Italy.

"Perhaps fastidious people might object to the temperature in summer, when the rays of the sun attain their maximum force, and the hot winds sweep in from the desert. It is said that a wicked soldier died here, and was consigned to the fiery region below for his manifold sins; but unable to stand the rigors of the climate, sent back for his blankets. I have even heard complaint made that the thermometer failed to show the true heat because the mercury dried up. Everything dries; wagons dry; men dry; chickens dry; there is no juice left in any thing, living or dead, by the close of summer. Officers and soldiers are supposed to walk about creaking; mules, it is said, can only bray at midnight; and I have heard it hinted that the carcasses of cattle rattle inside their hides, and that snakes find a difficulty in bending their bodies, and horned toads die of apoplexy. Chickens hatched at this season, as old Fort Yumers say, come out of the shell already cooked; bacon is eaten with a spoon; and butter must stand an hour in the sun before the flies become dry enough for use."

Actual fact: In the entire year of 1956, only .07 of an inch of rain fell at Davis Dam, 310 miles upriver from Yuma. Construction of the dam in the 1940s spawned Bullhead City, now a recreation boomtown and the hottest place in the United States during the 1980s.

It Doesn't Get Any Drier Than This

Not far inland from the river, a lost prospector perished of thirst in the desert near Quartzsite. Water had to be brought from the river to prime the mourners at his funeral. Baptisms in La Paz County churches won't wait for the end of a drought, so sometimes hard-shell Baptists spritz, and Methodists issue rain checks. Clergymen must rely on gentle persuasion; after a few summers on the desert, their parishioners have no fear of hell.

Back when Quartzsite was known as Tyson's Well, one of the local characters was a man called Scale Adams. His skin was so dry that friends struck matches on his hide, and sharpened their knives on his abrasive epidermis. One freaky day, a misplaced drop of rain hit Scale on the head and he passed out. His buddies had to throw sand in his face to revive him.

Idlers around Tyson's Well used to have spitting contests--not to see how far they could spit, but to see whether they could reach the ground. The fourteen trees that grow in modern Quartzsite strive to look inviting to passing dogs.

An Obligatory Passage From Martha

Martha Summerhayes actually saw soldiers die of the heat in the summer of 1874. She was a refined Nantucket girl who married an Army officer and accompanied him to Arizona that summer. She wrote a gushy, eloquent little book, *Vanished Arizona*, describing her hardships. Of course, she told the story about the soldier and his blankets.

No Arizona book is complete without a quote from Martha. In the summer of 1990, when the temperature reached 122 degrees in Phoenix, I found these passages describing travel on a steamboat as it labored up the Colorado River:

"But that dining room was hot! The metal handles of the knives were uncomfortably warm to the touch; and even the wooden arms of the chairs felt as if they were slowly igniting. After a hasty meal, and a few remarks upon the salt beef, and the general misery of our lot, we would seek out some spot which might be a trifle cooler...

"Conversation lagged; no topic seemed to have any interest except the thermometer, which hung in the coolest place on the boat; and one day when Major Worth looked at it and pronounced it one hundred and twenty-two in the shade, a grim despair seized upon me, and I wondered how much more heat human beings could endure."

Trains eventually killed steamboat traffic. In the days before air conditioned passenger cars, a westbound Southern Pacific train stopped in Yuma in midafternoon to take on coal and water. The cars baked in the sun and passengers sweltered. The only passenger who boarded at Yuma was a mournful-looking cowboy sucking on a sliver of ice, who was accompanying the remains of his friend back home to California.

"Where did you get that ice?" asked a passenger who was near heat stroke.

"You want some?" the cowboy asked. "I can get you some for fifty cents."

He took the four bits and walked off to the baggage car, returning soon with another sliver of ice. By now, nearly everyone in his car wanted ice, and he walked back and forth, delivering pieces of ice.

Only one person wasn't buying. "I'll be blamed if I'll pay fifty cents for ice," the man grumped. "It's robbery."

14

But when he saw everyone else happily sucking ice, the grouch told the cowboy he had changed his mind. He wanted some ice.

"Sorry," the cowboy said. "Can't do it. Not enough ice."

"What do you mean? You got ice for everyone else."

"Shorty won't keep."

Dick Wick Hall, a nationally-known humorist in the 1920s, wrote, "Yuma is the town where it is said a coyote walked down main street one summer afternoon chasing a jackrabbit, walking, both walking. Nothing ever runs in Yuma in the summer time, except molasses and the Colorado River, which is so full of mud it crawls."

Flora and Fauna of the Desert

The Colorado River may be "too thick to swim and too thin to plow," but at least it is moist. Visitors are sometimes startled to drive across bridges spanning Arizona "rivers" which have no water in them.

These dry streambeds used to be home to the sand trout, which burrowed through the sand much as his cousins swim through water. The best way to catch one was to troll with a horned toad on the end of your line. But a fisherman had to be wary, because a fighting sand trout might flip sand in his eyes. If the angler did succeed in dragging the trout from the sand, the fish emerged already scaled and cooked.

Sadly, the last known school of sand trout in Arizona was drowned by a flash flood in 1945.

Sand fishermen who couldn't find a horned toad often substituted a stick lizard for bait. The stick lizard is a protected species, but there's no law against taking one out for a walk. This adaptive creature looks like any common old lizard, but he carries a stick in his mouth. Every so often, he lays the stick down and climbs up on it so his feet can cool off. (The behavior I describe is that of the common Hassayampa stick lizard. The rare Gadsden stick lizard jabs his stick in the sand, climbs it and waves his extremities in the air to cool them.)

15

Graham

16

Arizonans learned from the stick lizards. Stationer John Wikle, who was five when his family moved to Tempe in 1909, says boys burned their bare feet in the sand while they were walking to a swimming hole in the Salt River for a cooling dip. They'd stop, set their straw hats on the ground and stand on the brims to cool their feet.

Some of the real flora and fauna of the desert are as amazing as the mythical ones. The tiny kangaroo rat hibernates for months or years, emerging only when it rains. A shrub called ocotillo puts out leaves to catch the rain, then sheds them so it won't lose moisture through transpiration. If the saguaro cactus was native to Alabama, rather than Arizona, it might be no bigger around than a broom handle. The fat saguaro sends out a broad, shallow root system to suck up from infrequent rains, and store it for the dry spells.

It is harder to document the behavior of the rare Mohave fenceweed. The ball-shaped plant has no roots and no leaves, so is free to roll endlessly across the desert, looking for a seep or a puddle left after a thundershower. Only a few patrons of a certain Wickieup tavern are capable of telling a live fenceweed from a dead tumbleweed.

Fenceweed can suck moisture from volcanic rocks, and survive for weeks on dew from a discarded Diet Sprite can tossed out by a passing litterbug. In other ways, however, the plant has not adapted well to the 20th century. It frequently is gulled by shimmering images of water on asphalt pavement, the most common mirage. If the fenceweed is not crushed by a passing 18-wheeler, it ends up jammed along a right-of-way fence along U.S. Highway 93.

Sometimes, the Only Relief is a Laugh

About 1906, Dick Wick Hall started a town named Salome in western Arizona. He named it for the wife of an investor, then made up a story about a tourist girl dancing like the Biblical Salome because she tried to go barefoot in the hot sand. Salome became two towns: the real place, and a mythical place that existed only in Hall's writings.

Hall started a business he called the Laughing Gas Station to serve tourists, and began using humor to sell gasoline, water, and oil. His occasional *Salome Sun* newspaper was "Made With a Laugh On a Mimeograph." Hall used random capital letters to avoid the monotony of so many small letters. Pretty soon *The Saturday Evening Post* started using his stuff, and he wrote a syndicated column. He was pretty famous before his untimely death in 1926.

Hall's trademark was his seven-year-old frog who hadn't learned to swim because there was no water around; the frog carried a canteen.

THE DESERT'S REVENGE

The fictional Arizona frog who carried a canteen was smarter than a man called Frog Edwards.

Edwards was one of the rowdier citizens of La Paz, a legendary gold mining camp that sprang up in 1862 on the Colorado River, 130 miles north of Yuma. La Paz died after the river changed its course in 1866-67.

Edwards was a southerner, and an ardent secessionist. One night in 1863, he fired on a group of Union soldiers who disembarked from a passing steamboat to seek recreation in La Paz. He killed two bluecoats and wounded two others.

Edwards vanished into the night, eluding pursuers as he headed toward Mexico. But he fled in such a hurry that he didn't take any water with him. Fate imposed a harsh justice--Frog Edwards was soon found dead of heat and dehydration.

Here's one of my favorite Dick Wick Hall yarns:

"Awhile back when the hot days were getting Warmed up Good and coming down the Home Stretch, I took the Thermometer over at the Laughing Gas Station and shoved the little tube up about Half a Inch so as to make it read 148 Degrees Hot when it only would have been about 130 in the Shade, just for Fun and to see what Imagination would do to some Folks.

"The Other Native who was working quit when he saw how hot it was and a Woman Tourist who came along just took One Look at it and Dropped Over in a Dead Faint. I looked in the Doctor Book to see what to do and as there wasn't any Cold Water handy I opened up her Collar and poured Eight bottles of Cold Strawberry Pop right out of the Ice Box down her Neck and just as I was Getting her Feet Up in the Air she Comes to and Liked to have Kicked my Head Off.

"Such Language! She looked like a Lady but she gave me the double devil, and not only wouldn't pay me for the 8 Bottles of Cold Strawberry Pop but she wanted me to pay Her for $37.00 worth of Pink Silk under Clothes she Said she had on and that I had Ruined and threatened to have me Arrested and Sue me for it or Them. I told her I was only following the Directions in the Emergency Doctor Book and that I Shut Both Eyes and never Looked when I poured it and she said she Believed That allright but what did I mean by trying to Get Her Money out of her stocking for if she hadn't Come to in time to Save it.

"I Wonder Where she had all that $37 Worth of Pink Silk that she Made such a Noise About and what anyone wants to wear So Much this Kind of Weather anyway. None of the Natives around here Never Do and I'll bet $37 would buy All the Under Clothes there is in This End of Yuma County, as Far as I ever see."

Another Arizona land promoter, who had not the strength of character that Hall had, located a mirage so attractive and persistent that he subdivided it and sold 112 lakeshore homesites at $12 down and $12 a month.

Weather scholar Robert Schmidli tells of the warm day in May when a tourist stopped for gas in the mining town of Ajo in southern Arizona.

"It sure gets hot in *Ay*-joe," he observed.

A Hispanic gas station attendant patiently explained that "j" is pronounced "h" in Spanish, so Ajo is pronounced "*Ah*-hoe."

The tourist replied, "I'll bet it really gets hot here in Hune and Huly."

One hot Huly day, a carload of European tourists stopped at the Dairy Queen ice cream franchise in Ajo to cool down. "How do you pronounce the name of this place?" one tourist asked the waitress.

Obligingly, she enunciated: "*Dare*-ee Queen."

Euphoric Tales of Beer and Instant Popcorn

There is a story told in the Midwest about the day it got so hot that popcorn popped in the fields. Cattle saw the mounds of white, thought it was snow, and froze to death.

Anyone who tries to tell that tale in Arizona is immediately suspected of being a rank newcomer. In the first place, summer heat would put seed popcorn in the "hazardous materials" category, and the construction of refrigerated bunkers for its storage would be prohibitively expensive. A bill introduced in the Arizona legislature last year would have banned the use of microwave popcorn by all but state-licensed handlers; left lying in the back seat of a car, an envelope of microwave popcorn can be deadly.

The other reason the popcorn gag doesn't work is that most cattle on Arizona's lower desert ranges rarely see water, much less snow. One country agent, newly arrived from Iowa, found a rancher filling barrels with water at a railroad water tank in Morristown. The county agent asked how far it was to the man's ranch.

"Five miles."

"Wouldn't it be more efficient to drill a well on your place?"

20

"Same distance, either way. Five miles."

That's one reason dehydrated water was developed some years ago in the Casa Grande area. The main benefit was a reduction in pumping costs, since it takes much less electricity to pump dehydrated water than wet water from deep wells.

Ranchers found that by growing cattle on dehydrated water, they could eliminate many of the costs of beef processing. They simply slice up a carcass and sell it directly to taverns as jerky.

Speaking of taverns, you probably think that light beer originated in Milwaukee in the 1960s or '70s. But light beer was discovered during Prohibition in the now-vanished mining town of Critter, Arizona. The gold mines at Critter didn't amount to much, but the town had the finest brewery of bootleg beer in Arizona. Then disaster struck: a prolonged heatwave dried up the town well.

Fortunately, the heatwave also created a vivid mirage, an inviting scene of a mountain lake. The brewers of Critter began to siphon water from the mirage and brew a fine, light, non-filling beer. The brew had only three calories per mug, and you could drink a keg of the stuff before you began seeing double mirages.

By the time it finally rained, Prohibition had been repealed. The town and the brewery disappeared, along with the recipe for the world's first truly light beer.

—CHAPTER 3—

DRY HEAT AND COSMETIC CLIMATOLOGY

One humid day I rode with a Montreal cab driver who knew only two things about Arizona: It is somewhere near California, and it has "dry heat."

Wherever I have been--Seattle, London, Baltimore-- people say, "Ah, it gets hot in Arizona. But it's a dry heat, I hear." I was at Churchill Downs in Louisville one day with a woman from Dallas who expanded on the theme: "Phoenix has a dry heat, and Dallas has a wet heat, and Louisville has a kind of soft heat."

Now, you have to appreciate that these people are trying to make polite conversation. After all, what does one say to an Arizonan? But the Arizonan hears it so often that it has become a bad joke, like Los Angeles smog and New York muggings. When a funnel cloud roared through one Phoenix neighborhood, a TV weatherman quipped, "Yeah, but it's a dry tornado."

If you are one of the new breed of adventurers who decide to visit Phoenix in summer, don't be surprised if the locals look pained when you mention dry heat.

It is true that Phoenix usually enjoys low humidity. Given the high desert temperatures, that is a very good thing. In fact, one reason temperatures go so high is that the sun doesn't have to heat an eastern-type load of moisture in the air. Nor is sunlight filtered by so much moisture.

A National Weather Service publication says nature has never allowed days of high humidity to coincide with days when the temperature gets above 105. Such a combination would be fatal to many people. The publication's author, longtime weather observer Robert J. Schmidli, wrote: "This is nature's way of not allowing conditions to get entirely out of hand."

For several years, dry heat has figured in the "heat index," the summer equivalent of the chill factor. Temperature and dewpoint (the temperature at which vapor forms, given a certain humidity) are incorporated on a scale that shows how hot 110 degrees "feels," according to some mythical and mystical average. One weatherman calls it the "sensible temperature," as opposed to the genuine temperature.

At the moment this is being written, the thermometer in Phoenix reads 108, but the relative humidity is 11 percent and the dewpoint 41, so the heat index says it only feels like 101 degrees outside. I have to admit that I have never felt so suffocated by 114-degree heat in Phoenix as I have by much lower temperatures in Orlando, Florida, or Washington, D.C. And when I venture east of the Texas panhandle, I miss the clear blue skies of the West, which lack the usual haze of other regions.

Dry Heat Generated Marvelous Propaganda

Arizona Territory needed a good many investors and settlers to realize its big dreams, and promoters began early to exploit the wonders of "dry heat."

In the desert valleys, a winter growing season allowed farmers to provide produce to eastern cities while northern farmers were still huddled around the stove reading the almanac. Winter farmers around Yuma still provide spring seed for farmers in colder climates.

As dams and canals were completed, promoters conducted massive campaigns to recruit "colonists." The Santa Fe and Southern Pacific railroads offered special, one-way "colonist" fares from Chicago and other major cities.

To attract newcomers, boosters downplayed the heat, in fact, they lied. Away back in 1884, Patrick Hamilton explained how other places did it in a thick guidebook, *Resources of Arizona:*

"Enterprising pioneers who are the fortunate owners of corner lots--which they wish to dispose of-- sometimes indulge a little exaggeration when speaking of the climate of their particular neighborhood. To induce migration and capital is the aim of these worthy citizens, and they do not stickle at facts when their interests are concerned. Though the malaria may rage for nine months in the year; though the cold may be so intense in winter that only an Eskimo can stand it; though cyclones, tornadoes and blizzards may be looked for every year; though the rain may come down with such persistent regularity that a glimpse of the sun is like a vision of Paradise, yet notwithstanding all these drawbacks, the sanguine settler will tell you that he 'never lived in a better climate,' and that the only mortality is caused by whiskey and six-shooters."

But not Hamilton. No, he was going to give the reader straight facts about the marvelous weather in Arizona. And he presented the most remarkable snow job about the advantages of Arizona's climatic regions. In fact, all his fine boasts for any one region were probably true for as much as 50 percent of any given year. Here's Hamilton's introduction to the climate of the desert:

"Snow rarely falls in the valleys, and the temperature for nine months in the year is unequalled for mildness, salubrity and healthfulness. While the heat during June, July and August is sometimes great, so dry, pure and exhilarating is the atmosphere that no injurious effects are experienced, and sunstrokes are unknown."

The Pacific Tourist, a detailed book published in 1884 to guide transcontinental railroad travelers, came nearer the truth: "Southern Arizona is delightful--the perfection of climate in winter, but excessively hot in summer . . ."

24

Early Phoenix newspapers ran page 1 roundups of the killer heatwaves that periodically swept the humid East. Local editors were incensed, however, when eastern editors sensationalized stories about the awful heat in Arizona. On July 14, 1897, Phoenix editor Charles C. Randolph reported: "The writer rode 53 miles across the desert Monday, with the thermometer indicating possibly 110 degrees, and suffered no inconvenience whatsoever. The absence of humidity and the fact that there is a breeze in the valley and on the surrounding mesas almost constantly, combine to make the temperature reports from this region very misleading."

It should be pointed out that Randolph had previously covered Washington, D.C., for *The New York Times*, and that may have caused some sort of brain damage.

In 1910, a Nebraska newspaperman recruited a party of colonists to Arizona. He compiled a long list of questions and answers for his charges, including this:

"Q: How is the climate of the Salt River Valley?

"A: The climate is mild...From June to September the weather is warm.

"Q: What is the average summer heat?

"A: About 87.7 degrees."

Perhaps he was referring to mean temperature, the midpoint between an average daytime high of 105.8 in July, and an average nighttime low of 81. The mean July temperature over 95 years has been 92.5.

In 1918, an investor from Pennsylvania succumbed to the literature of an Arizona land developer, and visited the Phoenix area in June. The developer's brochure admitted that it got warm in June, perhaps even uncomfortable. But even on the hottest days, there was an overnight "tang" in the morning air.

"And this is a hell of a tang in the air this morning," the Pennsylvanian said acidly to a newspaper reporter. "It's so damn hot it's ridiculous."

Hundreds of thousands of people were lured to Arizona, and they're still coming. Some may wonder, during their first couple of summers here, whether it was a wise move. Says Schmidli, a native of Milwaukee:

"This heat's not so bad up to 105 degrees. But when it gets up around 110, even the old-timers say it's too hot here. Still, it's easier to shovel 110 degrees than three feet of snow."

Taming Temperatures for a Legion of Immigrants

The promoters' optimistic view of Arizona weather became supportable after mechanical cooling was available. The advent of coolers coincided roughly with World War II. As that conflict loomed, boosters sold the federal government on the Arizona climate as a great place to train fighting men. So during the war, dozens of military training bases were established

BE CAREFUL WHERE YOU BUY A RANCH

For 35 years, I have listened skeptically as ranchers around Springerville complained about how little it rains there. But statistics bear out their sad story.

Springerville sits at about 7,000 feet elevation off the northeast shoulder of the White Mountains. Since winter storms come from the west and southwest, and summer storms from the south, mountain storms empty the clouds before they reach Springerville. Springerville averages only about 12 inches of precipitation a year, a little more than Tucson.

Payson is on the other side of the mountains, below the Mogollon Rim, nearly 2,000 feet lower than Springerville. Storms created by the Rim, and storms stalled by the Rim, drop their load on Payson. Three weather stations in the Payson area report from 22 to 30 inches of moisture from rain and snow in an average year.

After the war, there was a population explosion as former trainees migrated to Phoenix and Tucson, and others exercised a new mobility they had learned during the war. Population of the Phoenix metropolitan area rose from 331,000 in 1950 to 2.12 million people in 1990. But as Schmidli says, "There would be five million people here if it wasn't for excessive summer heat. It separates the desert rats from the sissies."

The summer business slump was no longer quite so severe, except in the tourist industry. So resort owners reverted to territorial-style propaganda with a "Summer's No Sweat" campaign, coupling the gentle untruth with room rates only half as steep as the winter rates.

Their slogan drew considerable scorn from seasoned observers like the author, who are inclined to estivate. I have already looked that word up for you: It means to pass the summer in a state of torpor, the Arizona alternative to hibernation.

But the new campaign seems to be working. An American Express survey of travel agents in 1991 showed that Phoenix had become the sixth most popular summer destination. People were taking advantage of low rates. They also were lured by proximity to Grand Canyon, Mexico and an unsurpassed collection of prehistoric ruins left by civilizations which dried up and vanished 800 years ago. Many summer tourists also were visiting family members who had been lured to Arizona by the great winters, or by great advertising brochures.

So now in summer, thousands of visitors cruise the air-conditioned boutiques, or hunker down in air conditioned resorts, and comfort each other with the old rallying cry:
"Yeah, but it's a dry heat."

—CHAPTER 4—

NIGHTLIFE ON THE LAWN

In June of 1892, restaurant chef William DeLou of Phoenix was sentenced to six months in jail for the heinous deed of stealing a friend's sleeping cot.

A newspaper said, "At that time of year when the hot weather was just coming on and indoor sleeping was an impossibility, the crime was considered an enormity, compared with which a bank burglary or a train robbery would have been considered an honest transaction."

In August, cooler heads prevailed. DeLou's sentence was commuted to time served.

Before mechanical cooling became commonly available in the 1930s, most residents of Phoenix, Tucson and smaller desert towns slept outdoors in summer. Their homes collected heat during the day, and were reluctant to give it up at night.

Native Americans had always lived summers outdoors, beneath "ramadas" or "coolers," which had brush roofs but no walls. Old, Spanish-type houses prevalent in Tucson and Yuma were designed to beat the heat. They had thick adobe walls, high ceilings and big doors and windows that could be opened up at night to let the hot air out.

But newer residents wanted homes like the ones they had known in older areas of the United States. And while Anglo women soon got over many of their eastern pretensions, they weren't ready for Mexican-style kitchens. So they built homes that trapped the heat.

Arizonans knew the principles of evaporative cooling, although they had not yet incorporated them into a cooling machine. When they went outdoors to sleep, some people wrapped up in wet sheets, and neighbors took turns sprinkling each other down. A Phoenix hardware store in 1910 listed the garden hose in its advertisement for "cooling devices."

People who could afford them added screened sleeping porches or balconies to their homes. The best hotel in Phoenix, Hotel Adams, had a "sleeping roof," as well as "suites." Each suite had an interior room reached from the hallway and a sleeping porch on a balcony overhanging the sidewalk. Owner J.C. Adams also experimented with cooling in the lobby, placing pans of ice around the floor and letting electric fans blow over them.

Graham

A cheaper hotel, the Jefferson, included a dormitory arrangement with wet sheets hanging down between the beds from overhead pipes.

About 1930, G.G. Skiles built one of the earliest residential swimming pools in Phoenix. That made the Skiles place very popular with neighbors and friends. At bedtime, the family put on its nightwear, jumped into the pool, then lay down on cots in a screened sleeping porch.

Men of means sent their families to the California coast or the mountains of northern Arizona, and commuted to these retreats on weekends; in the days before deodorants, only distance could take the worry out of being close.

Families who remained in Phoenix and slept outdoors lived a hazardous existence, especially after July 4. That's about the time of year when summer thundershowers arrived, often preceded by dust storms. According to this newspaper item from July, 1987, every night must have been Halloween: "There was great activity noted in all parts of the city early yesterday morning when white robed figures grasped blankets and mattresses and made haste to get under more substantial shelter than afforded by the leaky heavens. The rain poured down in torrents for a time and those sleeping out of doors were obliged to finish their nap indoors."

No one in town had any secrets from the newspaper carrier or the milkman, and neighbors developed a rare intimacy. An anthropologist friend has suggested tongue-in-cheek that the possibilities of lust on the lawn encouraged some men to send their families away for the summer; more later about "summer bachelors."

One of the worst invasions of privacy occurred to a man named Phillips, night telegraph operator for the Maricopa & Phoenix Railroad. He slept on a cot on the depot platform. Phillips wakened one morning to find his clothes and shoes missing. In their place was the ratty working uniform of a hobo, with this note in a pocket:

"Most Gracious Sir:

"To judge you from the benevolent and good nature that beamed from your face early this morning as I stood silently by your cot, I feel that you will forgive a poor, wandering man, who has been forsaken by his wife and children, and who has not tasted of whiskey for a week, through the want of the wherewith.

"I felt as I stood by your side and saw your clothing that I might once more become a gentleman. I picked them up and transferred them to my own person in an empty boxcar. I was about to throw my own duds away, but I reflected that you might need them yourself, so acting on the principle that a fair exchange does not constitute a robbery, I procured a newspaper and wrapped them up to place them under your cot.

"The bunch of keys and change I found in your clothes will be of use to me, but your suspenders I will return, so that you will have something to put on when you dress. Hoping you will not be inconvenienced, I will say adieu.

"(Signed) Restless Jimmie"

Phillips stayed in bed until an acquaintance fetched him some of his own clothes.

As much as possible, Arizonans stayed outside in the daytime, too. I overheard my mother telling my granddaughter how she survived summer afternoons when it was too hot to live in the house: "I took a chair outside, along with my sewing, or a book. I'd sit outside in the shade of a tree all afternoon, until it was time to go in and cook dinner."

Several entrepreneurs capitalized on the need for outdoor entertainment. Riverside Park at Central Avenue and the Salt River was a favorite spot for generations of Phoenix natives. It had a park, a swimming and diving pool, a dance pavilion, outdoor movies, a restaurant. Over the years, there were many other outdoor amusement parks, restaurants, dance pavilions. Buses and limousines ran regularly to recreation areas on Salt River.

Desert Rats Took Advantage of the Iceman

Phoenix got its first ice factory in 1879. Its proprietor, S.D. Lount, complained in 1897 that people were taking advantage of him. He had installed a drinking fountain outside his plant for the convenience of his customers. But some people were driving up in wagons and filling barrels with cold water so they could go home and take a nice, cooling bath. Lount said it was time "to draw the line."

MUMMIFIED LEFTOVERS

The author shares at least one idiosyncrasy with Payson author Marguerite Noble, a long-time observer of life in Arizona: We still call the modern refrigerator an "icebox."

Now I learn that "refrigerator" once was used to describe the old cabinet-type icebox, which used a block of ice to cool food.

Then came electric refrigerators. By 1934, the working parts had been removed from the top and hidden inside, and the sleek new machines were being merchandised aggressively.

Ice companies retaliated with a remarkable advertising campaign that suggested dire consequences from using electric refrigerators. "You wouldn't seal a fresh-cut rose in a fruit jar," Crystal Ice & Cold Storage Co. of Phoenix advertised, warning in another ad: "*Thirsty* air actually mum-mifies foods."

Diamond Ice Co. claimed, "Ice is the ONLY type of refrigeration that maintains correct humidity. It does not draw natural juices from foods but keeps them properly moist and fresh."

Later, there were five or six companies selling ice door-to-door by wagon, as well as manufacturing ice to chill refrigerated cars of produce headed for eastern markets.

Those were the days of the "cordless" refrigerator, or icebox, a cabinet of hardwood or metal, lined with tin and chilled by blocks of ice. The housewife left a sign in the window indicating how much ice she needed--25 or 50 pounds, usually. The iceman cut the block of ice to the proper size with a sharp ice pick, picked up the ice with vicious-looking tongs, and carried it right into the kitchen and installed it in the icebox.

A number of my older friends remember chasing the ice wagon, begging for the slivers of ice which flew from the iceman's pick. In Tucson, street vendors sold cones of shaved ice flavored with fruit juices. The Arizona Historical Society museum in Tucson displays a picturesque photo of vendor Juan Velasquez carrying a table full of syrup bottles balanced on his head.

Every town had its ice cream parlor, and most had local bottling works. In 1918, a Phoenix company tried to create mass demand for Celery-Vig, a cold drink made with celery juice. It never rivaled Coca-Cola.

Where ice was not available, desert-dwellers used the principles of evaporative cooling to keep milk relatively fresh and prevent butter from melting and running off the plate. A wooden frame was covered with burlap to make a porous "cabinet." A can or pan of water sat on top of the cooler. Water seeped from pinholes to the burlap. As water evaporated from the burlap, it cooled the cage and its contents.

Children in Phoenix, Tucson and Yuma might head for the nearest irrigation ditch to cool off. One popular Phoenix spot was a "falls" in the Town Ditch near Seventh Avenue and Polk Street. Yuma kids had the Colorado River, as dangerous as that was for a swimming hole, and a series of canals and ditches.

The sad fact is that there weren't that many ways to beat the heat. In the summer of 1918 *The Arizona*

Republican put together a special section on how to deal with the heat.

"How can a person keep cool?" one reporter wrote. "That is a foolish question, so a fool will try and answer it."

He tried again, lamely: "In Phoenix, where the weather is 100 percent, how to keep cool is an interesting subject."

Reporters came up with a pitifully short list of practical suggestions: Take cold baths. Drink cold buttermilk. Wear loose clothing and pith helmets. Use electrical appliances and oil stoves to keep the home from heating up in the first place. And eat lots of fresh, raw, locally-grown vegetables, made possible by the climate of Phoenix, thus avoiding heavy foods which had to be cooked.

It was some years later that President Harry S. Truman said, "If you can't stand the heat, stay out of the kitchen." He might have been referring to early Phoenix. The merchants who sold oil stoves, and later a growing array of electrical appliances, aimed their advertising at the guilt of husbands.

"To Men Only!" one ad began. "Suppose you had a wife and you could not afford to send her away during the hot summer months, and the little woman (or if she is a big woman, which makes it all the more suppositional) had to stay in the hot kitchen over a red hot cook stove to cook your three meals a day. So that about the time twilight came she was completely fagged out."

The message was that the kitchen stayed cooler with a Standard Wickless Blue Flame Oil Stove. Davidson's Cash Store, which advertised the oil stoves, offered a free fan of palm fronds to anyone who visited the store.

The electric iron also helped relieve husbands of their presumed guilt; it eliminated the need for flat irons, which had to be heated on the wood stove. Most homes were not wired for appliances. A 1910 advertisement noted that you could plug the Hotpoint iron ($4.25) into any socket "by removing the lamp."

CULINARY TIPS

Contrary to folklore, you cannot fry an egg on the sidewalk in Phoenix. Dozens of newspaper and TV reporters have tried. At 120 degrees, you can cook an egg on the surface of a black Honda Civic, but it ruins the paint. And most people like their eggs cooked more thoroughly.

We Arizonans pride ourselves on our chili. In summer I merely jump-start my red chili, called "World War III," then unplug the electric skillet and let the mixture simmer from its own heat for seven hours.

If I do not pull the plug, energy generated by the chili flows the wrong way and trips the circuit breaker, shutting down the air conditioning. You don't want to be caught in the same room with my chili when the air conditioning is off.

My Grampa Cook used to grow potatoes near Peoria and carry them 10 miles to Phoenix in a horse-drawn wagon. My Uncle Lawrence says that if Grampa left Peoria before dawn, he headed for the fresh produce markets. If he left around noon, he went directly to downtown restaurants and sold them ready-baked potatoes for the dinner trade.

Outdoor barbecuing, a summer activity elsewhere, is a winter sport around Phoenix. Barbecue tools come in handy in summer, however. A gardener or handyman can use barbecue mitts to pick up tools carelessly left lying in the sun. And a long-handled spatula is great for scraping up eggs that reporters have tried to fry on the sidewalk.

Yee Sing advertised that instead of heating up the home kitchen, a family should eat in his American

Kitchen restaurant. There four large fans were suspended from the ceiling by some sort of hinges, and connected with a single rod. During the worst of summer, an employe stood and moved the rod back and forth to fan diners.

Electric fans were available by the turn of the century, and people in rural areas could buy fans powered by kerosene or alcohol. But fans were expensive--in 1908 they cost $17 apiece, more than a week's wages for most people-- and they didn't do much good against the relentless heat of a Phoenix summer, when even sunflowers sought the shade.

"Steamy" Movies and Stage Shows Prevailed

Some early Phoenix theaters were outdoor affairs called "airdomes." They attracted every kind of traveling show from opera to trained dog acts, and later movies. Walls kept out the moochers, but the sky served as a roof.

Phoenix had indoor theaters, too. They employed electric ceiling fans, and handed out paper hand-held fans with advertising printed on them. But still the temperature could reach 125 degrees inside on a summer afternoon. The Columbia Theater was built with an elaborate cooling system that included an ice chute to a sub-basement. The iceman dropped ice into the chute from the street. Down in the depths, fans blew across the ice and forced cool air upstairs. Unfortunately, the air also was extremely humid.

L.N. Jesunofsky, the Weather Bureau observer stationed in Phoenix, took his wife and daughter to the Coliseum Theater one July night in 1910, during a series of 110-degree days. After the show, he found someone had stolen his horse and buggy. Newspapers speculated that the theft was (a) revenge, or (b) perpetrated by someone crazed by the heat wave.

An Anthropologist's Informal Assessment

Anthropologist Henry F. Dobyns gained an international reputation for his studies of Hispanic and Native American peoples. But Dobyns also offers some personal observations about how Arizonans beat the heat when he was growing up in Casa Grande. In 1936 his father built a home with a basement, a rarity in Arizona. It was used to store canned food and to make root beer for young Henry's soda pop deficiency, which we'll discuss a bit later. One summer an aunt and uncle came to visit.

"My aunt, a rather stout woman, was convinced that her heart was going to stop in the heat. My father and uncle did some rearranging of the basement shelving, carried a bed down and then half-carried my aunt into the basement. She never set foot out of the basement for the rest of the visit, except to climb the stairs to the bathroom--fortunately located right at the head of the stairway."

While old-timers laugh about it now, the effects of heat were sometimes serious. Young Dobyns was one of many Arizonans who had to be hospitalized because of the ill effects of heat. Fortunately, his doctor prescribed lots of soda pop to keep him from again becoming dehydrated.

But early newspapers are full of sad stories about heavy drinkers who didn't know, or didn't care, that alcohol actually speeds dehydration. Many died of heat stroke.

Old-timers say they did what they had to do to earn a living in summer, and tried to ignore the heat. The town was more open and airy then. There was less paving to absorb the heat, and fewer tall buildings to trap it.

Still, productivity declined, and so did commerce. In 1899 the Phoenix newspaper for which I work, now the largest in Arizona, almost went broke because advertisers couldn't pay their bills until their customers got back into town.

38

Families who couldn't afford to summer at the beach could at least load up the wagon or the Model T and go camping in the mountains which nature placed so conveniently throughout eastern and northern Arizona.

The Whispered Sins of "Summer Bachelors"

The truly fortunate families could afford a summer home in the Iron Springs enclave near Prescott, established by the leading families of Phoenix prior to 1900. During the 1920s and '30s, Tucsonans battled to get roads built up 9,120-foot Mt. Lemmon in the nearby Santa Catalina Mountains. A community called Summerhaven was built at the 8,000-foot level.

Other prosperous families took the train to the California shores, and had chauffeurs bring their automobiles to them. The Santa Fe, Prescott & Phoenix Railroad ran "Seaside Special" excursion trains to the Coast by way of Prescott, connecting with the Santa Fe in northern Arizona. The trip took 27 hours. The rival Maricopa & Phoenix, which connected with Southern Pacific, advertised that it's special excursion train would reach the Coast in only 16 hours.

Husbands who remained in Phoenix or Tucson or Yuma called themselves "summer widowers." But some acted like "summer bachelors," which is how they became known in scandalous folklore still whispered about today. There seemed always to be party girls who would keep a man from getting too lonely.

In 1904, one Phoenix newspaper printed this tongue-in-cheek pledge:

"Summer Widowers Association,
Headquarters City Hall Basement,
Phoenix, Arizona.

"Pledge: I hereby solemnly pledge myself to take within twelve hours of the departure of my lawful wife, a Summer Wife.

"I also promise never to 'blow the whistle' without due notice, and should I unknowingly do so, I pledge myself to obey the judgement of a three-fourths majority of the members of this association.

"Further, should I be caught without my fingers crossed, I agree to pay the fine set by the association, which is to be for all time, viz: the drinks for the crowd."

The newspaper's daily rival suggested that the attempt at humor was in poor taste, and perhaps dangerous. By listing the city hall basement, where police headquarters were located, the "pledge" might suggest to morally weak men that the police not only sanctioned adultery, but supplied women.

Old-timers still talk guardedly of the adventures of summer bachelors. But I suspect another man's experience was more typical of what happened to summer bachelors. The man wakened one morning after a night of partying and found the soles of his feet muddy. He couldn't remember being in mud, but then he couldn't remember much of anything. He hurried to the window to see if there had been a storm the night before, but the ground was dry.

Then he saw his footprints on the floor, and slowly realized what had happened. He had taken a bath before he went to bed, then walked across floors thick with weeks of accumulated dust.

He quickly set to work cleaning up the place before his wife and kids returned from Iron Springs.

—*CHAPTER 5*—

THE PAINFUL EVOLUTION OF THE SWAMP BOX

Every older Arizonan remembers where he was on Pearl Harbor Day, what he was doing when President John F. Kennedy was assassinated, and how he met his first evaporative cooler.

Way back on August 24, 1897, *The Hartford Courant* printed the famous line by editorial writer Charles Dudley Warner: "Everybody talks about the weather, but no one does anything about it."

Even then, that was not quite accurate. Textile manufacturers in the eastern United States had introduced moisture to clean the air in their mills, and found they also had "invented" evaporative cooling.

In 1902, Dr. Willis Carrier of Buffalo, N.Y., invented refrigerated air conditioning. That was a different animal, a system that would be beyond the means of most homeowners for half a century.

Meanwhile, the home-made, jury-rigged home evaporative cooler evolved slowly in the Southwest, apparently being "invented" in a number of towns. Cooler manufacturer Adam Goettl of Phoenix, who eventually held 100 patents in the cooling field, said, "The real inventor of evaporative cooling is Nature herself."

Arizona pioneers knew to hang a wet sheet on the back porch and let the wind blow cooling air into the kitchen, or hang a wet dish towel on the back of a chair and let an electric fan blow through it. Between 1900

41

and the early 1930s, handymen tried a thousand different ways to mate evaporation with an electric fan, hoping to devise a contraption that would blow cool air without causing hearing loss or spattering water all over the wallpaper.

"They had some awful-looking contraptions," Phoenix civic leader Tom Chauncey said. "Boxes, wooden crates full of holes, wires, water, any kind of fan." A.C. Williams, a native of Phoenix, said his family's first evaporative cooler was powered by the gasoline engine from a Maytag washing machine.

Since most homes had no built-in ductwork, the coolers were usually installed in a window, and wet down by garden hoses tied in place with baling wire. Chauncey said that in the late 1920s, the owner of a Phoenix cafe cut a large hole in the end wall of his establishment and used a fan to draw air through a large pad of wet horse hair.

Graham

"He did a hell of a business," Chauncey recalled. Chauncey built a noisy swamp box for the rectory at St. Mary's Catholic Church, using the noisy squirrel-cage fan from a Franklin automobile. "It whistled so you heard it all over town, but you didn't mind the noise if you were cool."

Chauncey thought briefly about going into the business of manufacturing evaporative coolers. Instead, he became a successful jeweler, television station owner and Arabian horse breeder.

One major problem with manufacturing a compact cooler was what sort of medium to use to spread the water out so the fan could draw air through it. People tried using metal plates to evaporate the water, but they corroded. So did steel or zinc shavings. Charcoal clogged up with sediment. Wet horsehair didn't smell good. Sawdust just packed down and got soggy.

Finally, the makers of evaporative coolers settled on excelsior, thin wood shavings, usually packed between layers of chicken wire. In early homemade coolers, this moisture medium was tacked around a box-like wood frame. A fan inside the "swamp box" forced air through the wet sides.

By the early 1930s, quite a few workable evaporative coolers were showing up around Arizona. Cliff Harkins, later Arizona's state superintendent of public instruction, said he was a grade school teacher in Yuma when he heard of the first evaporative cooler, installed on the home of a barber. "I let my kids out of school and we all went over to see it," he said.

John H. Wikle, auditor for Arizona State Prison at Florence, lived on the prison grounds in the 1930s. He said convicts built him an evaporative cooler using coke as an evaporator. "It sort of cooled the air part of the time," Wikle said.

The J.C. Penney store in downtown Phoenix installed a large swamp cooler in 1929, and it blew a cool draft out the front door. "Loafers used to hang around Penney's in the afternoons, trying to keep cool,"

Phoenix native Charlie Mann says. "People would say, 'I'll meet you at Penney's.' "

About then, or maybe slightly earlier, Korricks Department Store built a crude evaporative system, using a wall of some sort of porous material. Around 1930, the store upgraded its "air conditioning" by installing in its cooling room an old York ice-making machine, originally used in ice factories. Fans from the evaporative system blew air over the ice and into the store. Former Phoenix City Council member Ed Korrick says he's too young to remember the genesis of the system, but he can still hear the rhythmic beat of the old ice-maker.

Retired businessman Jay O'Malley said Goldwater's department store across the alley from Korricks had no cooling. During slack times, employees from Goldwater's slipped across the alley to rib the Korricks employes about being pampered, and coincidentally to enjoy the cool air at Korricks.

Yuma mechanic and lawyer J.A. Eddy built some of the first coolers around Yuma. Some publications have credited Phoenix radiator shop owner Oscar Palmer with "inventing" evaporative cooling. More accurately, Palmer was an innovator. In the spring of 1934 he started manufacturing the Sno-Breeze brand cooler in his Phoenix shop. Palmer ran a contest for a slogan, and adopted this grand-prize winner: "Keeps heat outside."

Refrigerated Air Comes to Arizona

Meanwhile, refrigerated air conditioning reached Phoenix commercial establishments in the 1920s. In fact, some experimental units were manufactured in Phoenix as early as 1925. Home air conditioning was displayed at a Phoenix home show in 1935, but the machines were beyond the reach of most people until the 1950s or later.

Both the Fox and Orpheum theaters, which opened in 1929, soon had some sort of air conditioning system.

Salesmen were seen to glance surreptitiously up and down Washington Street to see if anyone was watching, then slip into the Fox for a matinee. That same year, air conditioning was installed at the new telephone company office and the Hotel Westward Ho. In 1937, Dr. Carrier air conditioned a copper mine at Superior, Arizona, to bring the temperature down from 140 to 93 degrees.

Meanwhile, the "swamp box," the evaporative cooler, was catching on. A Phoenix newspaper reported that as of January, 1935, there were few commercially-built evaporative coolers in the city; by the spring of 1936, the business was booming. By the end of 1936, 5,000 Phoenix homes had coolers. Homebuilders began building in ducts to carry cool air throughout new houses.

The Cooks were not of the economic class that could afford a swamp box. As I wrote earlier, we solved our cooling problems by gypsying north in summer. But my grandfather was janitor at Washington Elementary School near Phoenix (now in Phoenix), and lived in a little house on the school grounds. This house had a traditional screened sleeping porch with canvas flaps that rolled down in winter, or during a dust storm.

Then the school district installed an evaporative cooler in a living room window of my grandparents' house. It was still hot when we returned to the Phoenix area from the mountains each September, and I luxuriated in the cool air at Grandpa's house. I thought school janitors must be among the most privileged people in society.

The old evaporative cooler was not without its shortcomings. Its cabinet tended to rot or rust. Sometimes the cooler stank. Pads had to be changed every year or two. And when the humidity doubled in July and August--when the dewpoint reached 55 or so-- evaporative cooling was not nearly so effective.

I quit Phoenix altogether for 21 years. When I returned, homes had refrigerated air conditioning. Refrigeration units and heat pumps take the moisture from the air and drain it outside. And the cost of running refrigeration wasn't so bad back in the 1960s-- maybe $60 a month during a really hot August.

The main problem with refrigeration is that it tends to break down at the most awkward times--the Friday night of a three-day weekend, or the day of your daughter's wedding. Late in the 1960s, we returned dirty and tired from a family camping trip to find that the refrigeration had died. What did we do? We slept on the lawn, just as people had in 1907.

Then came the oil crisis of the 1970s, along with constantly increasing inflation. The cost of electricity went sky high, and many people went back to swamp coolers, usually in tandem with a heat pump or an air conditioner.

Mechanical cooling allowed Arizona to become as productive as other states in the summertime. And they made it possible for hordes of new people to migrate to the Southwest after World War II. Washington School was the only school in its district when I used to loll beneath Grandpa's swamp box; now there are 32 schools in the district.

Yet in some ways, things have not changed that much. Many people still flee to the California coast for vacation. Most go to San Diego, where they are called "Zonies" now instead of "Hassayampers." And residents of Phoenix and Tucson have created several substantial summer home communities in the mountains of Arizona.

The latest trendy gadget is the mister, a series of jets which spray a fine mist around patios, pools and outdoor restaurants. So people who huddled indoors for half a century now use evaporative cooling in order to spend more time living outdoors, as they did in 1910.

SOLAR LASSITUDE

Important research in solar energy has been conducted in Arizona. It hasn't captured the imagination of Arizonans, who equate the sun's power with a loss of energy.

Pioneers used solar energy in several devices, including the solar clothes drier, a line of rope or wire between two poles. They called it a "clothesline."

Seriously, solar-powered water pumps were used on Arizona farms early in this century. Many homes had efficient solar water heaters on their roofs. These devices disappeared as new sources of energy became readily available: natural gas for heating water, electric motors and internal combustion engines for pumping water.

During the early 1970s, when petroleum prices soared, rooftop water heaters enjoyed new popularity. Water heating contraptions still grace the roofs of Arizona homes, adding their ungainly lines to the accumulated heat pumps and piggy-backed evaporative coolers.

Arizona also enjoyed a new dawn of research into the solar generation of electricity in the 1970s. Then oil prices fell, and interest waned again.

It was probably just as well. In the 1970s, researchers found that experimental electrical generation plants could operate only at night; during the day, solar collection panels had to labor to keep up with the sunlight. And lighting the plants for nighttime research consumed most of the electricity they produced.

—CHAPTER 6—

ROLL DOWN THE AIR CONDITIONING

Westerners quickly became infatuated with horseless carriages, which were ideal for eating up vast distances in their part of the country.

But summer travel was arduous, to say the least. Radiators boiled, fan belts broke, tempers snapped, and tires lasted no time at all. Water and gasoline were hard to find, so motorists had to carry a supply.

A race driver or an automobile dealer might make a "speed run" from Phoenix to the California coast in 20 hours, but families escaping Arizona heat took as long as five days to make the trip. When four prominent and adventuresome Phoenix families made the trek west in convoy in 1918, they hired a mechanic to accompany them.

Headlights were not standard equipment at first, but as they became available, many people traveled at night. In June, 1918, Richard "Chevrolet Dick" Hollingsworth, a roving factory representative for that motor company, set out on a "speed run" from Phoenix to Los Angeles. But when Hollingsworth reached the Colorado River at 3 a.m., he encountered a stubborn ferryman who refused to take him across the river until 7 a.m. That ruined his attempt at a new record. Worse still, it cost him four hours of cool driving.

Frances D. Nutt, who compiled all the writings of Dick Wick Hall into a book, *An Arizona Alibi,* remembers traveling between Arizona and California when she was a girl. Her father would buy a block of ice in El Centro and put it on the floor by the back seat. Fran cooled her stockinged feet on the ice, while wind whipping over it cooled the car's interior a few degrees.

In his foreword to Nutt's book, former U.S. Senator Barry Goldwater told of spending two-and-a-half to five days traveling to the Coast when he was a boy. His dauntless mother, Josephine, stocked up on gas and water at Salome, and wherever else she could. I don't know if Hall charged for water, but my maternal grandfather, Jim Dodson, had to pay 5 cents a gallon at Desert Center, California.

Watching for Sunburned Left Elbows

Cars and roads improved over the next half century, but for most Arizonans, automobile air conditioning still meant rolling down the windows and driving fast. Water was carried in a canvas water bag hung from a door handle or radiator ornament.

Packard Motor Company came out with the first automobile air conditioning in 1939, but who (except doctors) could afford it? The Arizona Historical Society's museum in Tucson exhibits the door from a 1956 Nash. To its window is attached a cannister-like Kool Air evaporative car cooler, built in Phoenix. A turbine caught the air as the car sped down the road and spun it into the interior of the car. A placard with the exhibit suggests the cooler was a life-saver, but I don't remember them working very well.

Travelers who had no coolers rolled down the windows, opened the wind wings, and rested their arms on the door. A long-distance driver developed a sunburned left arm which we natives identified as "tourist elbow."

Nowadays, nearly everyone has factory air. While I haven't had a sunburned left arm in years, I suffer a modern malady. I turn my air on high and drive for quite a while before I notice how cold the car's interior has become. Then I find my right arm has goosebumps, and maybe a bone-deep chill, from the draft of air conditioning. I call it "summer elbow syndrome."

DRY SPOKES

When early travelers found a pool of water, they backed their wagons into the water to allow wooden wheels to soak up moisture. Otherwise, the dry wood shrank away from the iron tires.

Early in the 20th century, when automobiles had wheels with wooden spokes, Phoenix residents backed their Studebakers into the Arizona Canal for a good soak.

There is no such remedy for the windshield wiper blade, which dries out quickly in the desert air, and scrapes maddeningly across the glass when it does rain. Meticulous motorists change blades every six months, but some blades wither and die without ever wiping away rain water. Only an occasional visit to a car wash reminds them of their calling.

Sometimes in summer I see a frustrated person driving a black automobile with the windows down--a person sweating heavily, with an angry look on a red face. (I feel even sorrier for insecure people who drive around with the windows rolled up because they don't want anyone to know they have no air conditioning. The temperature inside a closed automobile can quickly surpass 145 degrees.)

The car may have Arizona license plates, but if I look closely, I can find a dealer's logo from somewhere in the upper Midwest or New England. Odds are it has vinyl seatcovers.

I know that (1) another newcomer is about to become a naturalized Arizonan (2) a lucky car salesman is about to sell aforementioned immigrant a light-colored car with factory air, tinted glass and fabric upholstery. Dark colors absorb heat; light colors reflect heat. Vinyl upholstery doesn't "breathe" as fabric does; it seems to adhere to human skin while it cooks the underlying flesh.

For many years, only physicians had covered parking, usually carports reserved for them outside clinics and hospitals. It has been rumored that sons of physicians sometimes followed their fathers into the profession simply to have covered parking. But then some real estate in Phoenix and Tucson became too expensive to be used for parking lots, so parking garages became popular.

For those who still have to park in the sun, other remedies are available: a towel over the steering wheel, or one of those cute sun shades, printed with sunglasses or a political message, to deflect the sun coming through the windshield. (Many of those devices had "Help! Call Police" printed on the flip side. As motorists grew careless about which side they displayed, some parking lots began to look like scenes of mass distress.)

Blocking the windshield does not solve the problem of blistering hot door handles and seat belt buckles. In *You Know You're An Arizona Native...*(Prickly Pear Press), contributor Melanie Johnson wrote: "You know you're an Arizona native when you order the 'Arizona Package' for your new car and get (1.) air conditioning, (2.) tinted glass, (3.) barbecue mitts."

—CHAPTER 7—

COMPETING FOR DUBIOUS DISTINCTION

You may have heard Bullhead City, Arizona, mentioned on the evening weather news and wondered how the town got its homely name. Are its citizens especially obdurate? Or does it have a bumper crop of the nasty little stickers known as "bullheads?"

As a matter of fact, Bullhead City was named for a large rock, shaped like the head of a bull. The rock disappeared under Lake Mohave when Davis Dam was built on the Colorado River in the 1940s. Bullhead City started as a construction town for the dam, but now it's a sprawling boomtown, fueled by the gambling casinos of Laughlin, Nevada, directly across the river, and by visitors who use the river as a playground.

During the decade of the 1980s, Bullhead City reported the nation's hottest temperature more than 360 times, outsweating any other town in America. That's according to *Weatherwise* magazine, which keeps track of such things. Bullhead's all-time record high was 126 on June 28, 1984.

That doesn't mean Bullhead is the hottest place in the nation: Death Valley, California, is usually hotter, but *Weatherwise* excludes Death Valley from its annual rankings precisely because it is so uncommonly hot. Fame is a fickle thing. In 1990, Bullhead City's 22 national maximums dropped it into a four-way tie with nearby Lake Havasu City and Yuma, both on the Colorado River, and McAllen, Texas.

Fame of any kind is useful to a place like Lake Havasu City, a planned community and resort where part of the old London Bridge was reconstructed in the 1960s. Lake Havasu City tied with Laredo, Texas, for the most national highs (34) in 1986. Its economy relies heavily on recreation along the river, and on winter visitors.

Curiously, two of Arizona's traditional hot spots, Parker and Gila Bend, don't fare well in the recent, masochistic national rankings. Parker, another Colorado River recreation port, has reported Arizona's highest maximums for three months out of the year, and tied for the heat record in two other months.

If you want to know how fickle fame can be, ask the residents of Gila Bend. The usually-dry Gila River makes a big bend between Phoenix and Yuma.

The Butterfield Stage used to pass this way; now Interstate 8 and U.S. 80 join here, merging California-bound traffic from Phoenix and Tucson.

During pre-Interstate days, when car cooling systems had to work harder to make it across the desert, Gila Bend called itself "The Fan Belt Capital Of The World." You could buy a coffee mug which proclaimed Gila Bend the hottest town in America.

Until June 26, 1990, Gila Bend's official record high had been 121 degrees; on that date, it was one of several Arizona stations to report 122. Local people swear their unofficial thermometers sometimes read as high as 127.

In 1987, the National Weather Service made the local weather observer switch from an alcohol thermometer to an electronic thermometer, and the official temperature readings dropped by several degrees. That did not sit well with the official weather observer, motel owner Duke Fox, who also was mayor of Gila Bend. He said the new thermometer was inaccurate. (The NWS has since admitted that some of its pricier electronic thermometers err, but on the high side, not the low.)

Fox was openly skeptical of Bullhead City's emerging status. He complained that the Bullhead thermometer had been moved from place to place in order to rig the temperature.

"For years and years, Bullhead City was never the hot spot in the nation, and then all of a sudden it was," Fox said. "Bullhead City has taken it over."

Bullhead City's official thermometer has been moved three times, in fact. But its reported temperatures may be rigged to appear lower than they are. In 1989, an official at the National Climatic Data Center in Asheville, N.C., admitted that the National Weather Service was averaging temperatures from two observation points in Bullhead, hoping for a realistic reading; the second reading frequently was lower than that of the "official" thermometer behind the fire station. (Bullhead's firemen, who keep an eye on the official thermometer, are frequently seen huddling next to burning buildings to enjoy the relative cool.)

Reports of the rigging caused some friendly arguments between those who think Bullhead's reports are too high, and those who think they're too low.

Proponents of the higher readings point to Laughlin, separated from Bullhead only by the width of the river. Laughlin is frequently the hottest place in Nevada, and in 1989 was the fourth-hottest place in America. I personally investigated the climate of Laughlin four times during 1989. While I spent little time outside the air-conditioned casinos, I found that (1) it is indeed hot in Laughlin (2) there was no apparent correlation between temperatures and my luck, which ran at near-record low.

On the surface, this competition to be miserable seems ridiculous. But just the other day, Lake Havasu City reported the nation's high, 118, and a low the following morning of 92. Darned if I didn't feel a bit of reflected local pride.

A resident of forsaken Gila Bend explained it succinctly to a newspaper interviewer in 1988: "Everybody needs to be proud of something. It's hot here, so we're proud of it."

—CHAPTER 8—

WE CAN'T REMEMBER THE
LAST TIME IT RAINED

The book of Genesis tells how, in the time of Noah, it rained 40 days and 40 nights. The great flood covered the earth to a depth of 15 cubits above the mountaintops.

Oral tradition says that Arizona only got 1.75 inches of rain out of that storm, less than a tenth of a cubit. (A cubit is the distance from elbow to finger tips. Assuming that Noah wore a 16-33 dress shirt, he would have used an 18-inch cubit.)

That is not to say that Arizona never had a flood. It has had many. The history of the Southwest is a story of monotonous, cloudless days interrupted by catastrophic exceptions.

One effect of aridity seems to be expungment of memories as brain cells dry out. The average Arizonan will tell you he can't remember the last rain. *Climate of Arizona*, published by the University of Arizona in 1985, sampled damaging storms over the previous century. There were an astonishing number of recent floods I should have remembered but didn't. Most Arizona floods occur so suddenly that Noah would barely have time to grab a life vest; forget building an ark.

Let's not get too precipitously into the subject of precipitation, for we first need to understand Arizona in its normal condition, which is without much water. In one recent year, Arizona ranked 40th among the 50 states for the number of storms per 10,000 square miles. I am writing this chapter in July. On July 20, 1991 .13 hundreds of an inch of rain ended a string of 114 days with no measurable precipitation in Phoenix. Had it not been for abnormal March rains--10 inches in 24 hours in some places on the Salt River watershed-- Phoenix might be rationing water now.

You Have to Give Arizona Rivers Some Latitude

You'll see several rivers on an Arizona map, but most of them have become largely ceremonial--every state ought to have a few rivers. American explorers of the 1840 and '50s noted in their journals that some Arizona rivers would be mere creeks back East. In fact, creeks in Arizona are more likely to contain water than are rivers.

Some rivers, like the Little Colorado and the Santa Cruz, start out with water in them but soon vanish into sandy, porous beds. Larger streams have been dammed, partly because of their seasonal nature. Some streams flow along, unseen, beneath a dry riverbed.

Driving to Tucson recently, we traversed one of the long bridges that carry Interstate 10 across the Gila, ranked as one of the major rivers of the Southwest. Our six-year-old granddaughter looked at the broad wash filled with Mesquite trees and creosote bushes and asked, "This is a river?"

The Gila never carried much water, even before it was dammed. But in the 1880s, the flooding Gila repeatedly washed out bridges on the only railroad to Phoenix. When a new bridge was built in Florence, the Gila promptly cut a new channel around the bridge. The flooding Gila is still not to be trifled with.

The Salt River through the Phoenix area used to run so low that it starved farmers out in some seasons. Then it flooded them out during the rainy seasons, periodically devastating the young farm town.

So Roosevelt Dam was completed 55 miles upstream in 1911 to provide a reliable supply of irrigation water, and that started the Phoenix area toward becoming a metropolis. (It also saved farmers from flood and drought as early as 1910, the year before it was dedicated.)

Because of Roosevelt, and subsequent dams, the bed of the urban Salt is usually dry, except when it floods and cuts the metropolis in half. When one Arizonan returned from his first visit to New York, a friend asked him what he thought of the Hudson River.

"Couldn't tell much about it, " he said. "It was full of water the whole time I was there."

The Santa Cruz runs north through Tucson. An old joke there says the ice on the Santa Cruz breaks up the first day the temperatures reaches 100. In the 1880s, a fancy resort hotel opened at Calabasas, south of Tucson. An imaginative San Francisco printer earned a place in Calabasas history when he printed up a brochure showing a steamboat chugging up a fancied Santa Cruz toward the hotel.

In its normal condition, the Santa Cruz would not float a tree leave. But when the river floods, head for high ground, especially if you live on the west side of Tucson. The Santa Cruz had a record flow, in October, 1977, when remnants of Tropical Storm Heather pumped moisture into the region.

All this aridity can mislead a casual visitor to Arizona. He sees expensive bridges over dry washes, with signs identifying the Salt or the Gila. And he sees signs where highways dip through other washes warning, "Do not Cross When Flooded."

And he thinks, "Are you kidding me?"

Not at all. The only place they're kidding is where a bridge crosses the usually bone-dry Hassayampa River at Wickenberg and a sign warns: "No Fishing From Bridge."

Legend says he who drinks from the Hassayampa will never tell the truth again. In fact, he who drinks from the Hassayampa has to travel to the Bradshaw Mountains, where it is a sparkling creek; by the time it gets down to Wickenberg, it's a sandy wash. Yet the Hassayampa has produced some of the most devastating floods in the history of Arizona, and especially in the history of Wickenberg.

For eventually, in every part of Arizona, it will rain. Phoenix averages 7.11 inches a year, and Tucson 11.14 inches. Yuma averages only 2.65 inches a year, but the Payson area, which straddles 5,000 feet elevation, averages 20 to 30 inches a year, some snow, mostly rain.

During a mostly sunny winter, a series of eastbound storms from the Pacific will pass over Arizona. Most of these storms drop their moisture in California, west of the Pacific Slope, and don't have much left for Arizona. But sometimes they hold their water until they get over Arizona, where they are stalled by a high pressure system parked to the east.

The Arizonans become festive. While people in gloomier climates dread rain, residents of the Arizona desert long for moisture, and not just because its needed: rain breaks up the monotony. But if the winter rain continues for very long, you'd better send someone to warn people downstream, especially if the rain falls on the remnants of a snowpack in the higher mountain regions.

During dry spells, oily residue from automobile exhausts build up on the streets of Phoenix and Tucson. Mix in water from the occasional rain, add wet breaks and dry windshield wipers, and dial 9-1-1.

Women of Phoenix used to use silk parasols to protect against the sun, but umbrellas were unknown here until the last few years. Now umbrellas have become fashionable. Few things are more dangerous than a native Arizonan with an umbrella, trying to open it in an elevator or close it after he gets into the cab of his pickup truck.

THE FABLED HASSAYAMPA

No Arizona river carries so little water or so much folklore as the Hassayampa. It begins as a mountain creek south of Prescott and ends as a dry wash joining the equally dry Gila southwest of Phoenix. Its name came from Hualapai Indian words meaning "place of water and big rocks."

Gold was discovered along the Hassyampa in the 1860s. Soon, prospectors there were being called "Hassayampers," a name that eventually became synonymous with "Arizonan." Arizonans who fled to the California shore in summer had a Hassayampa Club that met there.

Occasionally the Hassayampa has a mood swing and washes away everything in its path. No one is sure whether the river got its reputation from its unpredictability, or from the lies told by prospectors.

One legend says that if you drink from the waters of the Hassayampa, you never tell the truth again. A more complex myth says that if you drink facing upstream, you will always return to the Hassayampa; if you face downstream, you will never tell the truth again.

This bit of territorial doggerel embraced both philosophies:

You've heard about the wondrous stream
They call the Hassayamp.
They say it turns a truthful guy
Into a lying scamp.

And if you quaff its waters once
It's sure to prove your bane.
You'll ne'er forsake the blasted stream
Or tell the truth again.
Orick Jackson

The Robust Storms of the Arizona Monsoon

The real storms, however are likely to come in summer. Then air currents rotate up through Mexico in a counterclockwise motion, dragging up moist air out of the Gulf of Mexico and the Gulf of California, triggering violent thunderstorms and intense rain. As Arizona has become more pretentious, these have come to be called "Monsoon" storms (see the accompanying explanation at the end of this chapter).

Storms circulate into southern Arizona about two weeks before they reach the northern regions. Desert Indians believe the summer rains begin a week or two after locusts begin to sing, or around San Juan's Day, June 24. Up north, we used to figure the rains started about July 4. In the north, Hopis hold their sacred, private snake dance to bring the summer rains, and their timing seems to be good. I have read that Navajos call these "male rains," as opposed to the gentle female rains of winter.

The Mogollon Rim is an escarpment which rises 2,000 feet above the Tonto Basin in central Arizona. Its summit averages 7,500 feet elevation, and it forces moist monsoonal air upwards quickly, speeding the mixing of warm and cool air that leads to thunderstorms. Thus, it has a profound effect on the weather and the water supply for much of Arizona, including the Phoenix area. The Rim also generates some of the scariest thunderstorms in Arizona.

As a boy living at an isolated cabin atop the Rim, I remember lying on my back watching a single wisp of cloud form in a sky that had been absolutely clear all through June, Arizona's sunniest month. The only sound was the sighing of the wind in the pines, a whisper we didn't even notice anymore.

Within hours, my single wisp of cloud had become towering thunderheads, silver at the top, dark and threatening at the bottom. Just before the cloud blew out at the bottom, the air became so still that it even silenced the sighing of the pines. Then came a thunderstorm, frequently accompanied by the kind of intense rain my Dad called a "gulley-washer."

Newcomers may expect to find lost gold at the foot of every rainbow. What they frequently encounter, however, is a flash flood.

A number of summer storms drop a surprising amount of water in a short time. The water gathers in mountain canyons and desert washes and heads downstream at a high rate of speed, gathering force as it goes. It also gathers in urban canyons and washes--the streets of Phoenix, Tucson and other cities.

Tucson's Record Frog Strangler

The first mention of a major Arizona storm in government weather records told of a cloudburst July 11, 1878, when 5.10 inches of rain fell at Tucson within two hours, still an unofficial record for any two-hour period in the city and state.

Richard A. Wood, a retired National Weather Service meteorologist who was in charge of the Tucson weather bureau a century later, has done much research on that storm. He said high-level weather observations were not possible until much later, so it's hard to tell what caused the storm. But he cites newspaper accounts which tell of the apparent collision of two thunderstorms, traveling in opposite directions. He suspects that moisture from a tropical storm off the coast of Mexico may have been sucked up by a large storm circulating out of the Pacific Northwest. The same storm drenched much of southern Arizona territory and southern California.

Whatever the causes, a Tucson newspaper reported, "Soon the streets of Tucson leading to the bottom lands were a roaring sea of water. Buildings were washed out, walls torn down, and families were fleeing for safety in great alarm . . . It was a vast ocean between main street and the mountains on the opposite side of the (Santa Cruz River) bottom. . . The storm lasted about three quarters of an hour (it actually lasted from 4:45 to 6:30 p.m., but some of the rain was light) and rain fell to a depth of six inches on the level."

In the southeastern corner of Arizona, the storm killed two Army officers who were riding their horses through a canyon in the Chiricahua Mountains when a wall of water overtook them. Yet at Fort Lowell, six miles northeast of downtown Tucson, there was not a drop of rain.

There have been hundreds of damaging floods since that time. In 1881, a flood on the Hassayampa River devastated mining towns and farms, and killed several people. Nine years later, Walnut Grove Dam on the upper Hassayampa collapsed during heavy rains. That flood killed upwards of 60 people, and eradicated all signs of one mining community.

"The City Hall Bell Was Ringing Wet"

When a flood devastated Phoenix in 1891, merchants tried to stifle one newspapers report of damage, so it wouldn't scare off investors. When another flood hit Phoenix early in 1897, the editor of *The Arizona Republican* wrote two columns of satire, likening the towns flooded streets to a busy harbor. He headline it "Shipping Intelligence," and noted, "The city hall bell was ringing wet yesterday."

Many Arizonans remember the Labor Day weekend of 1970. Twenty-three people died when heavy rains flooded mountain canyons in the Payson area, then roared on down the drainages of the Salt and Verde rivers. At Workman Creek, north of Globe, rain totalled 11.40 inches in 24 hours, a record for the state.

When rain fills the major irrigation reservoirs on the Salt and Verde rivers, officials of the Salt river project have to release water into the Salt. It roars through Phoenix, blending with runoff from the city itself. Several times in the 1970s and '80s, most notably in 1980, bridges and crossings were washed away and the Phoenix metropolitan area was cut in half.

Arizona floods are rated in terms of probable frequency: a 100-year flood is of a volume and strength that should occur only once every 100 years. Somewhere in Arizona there were one or more 100-year floods in 1978, 1979, 1980 and 1983.

I have been washed downstream by one mild flash flood, and cut off from civilization by another. They make cute stories now, but when it's happening, a flash flood is as about as much fun as a tax audit.

Most weather-related deaths in Arizona result from someone driving in a mountain canyon or a desert wash. Inevitably, someone tries to outrun a wall of water running through a steep canyon, or ignores the warnings about crossing desert washes. Only a lucky few survive.

Either desert washes are not as shallow as they appear, or they mischievously sink when they fill with water. One Good Samaritan was getting ready to throw a rope over the head and shoulders of a man struggling against the swift waters of a flooded river wash in northwest Phoenix.

"How deep is it?" he called.

"Pretty deep. I'm standing on my pickup."

Within hours the water recedes. In a few days, the cemetery is dry enough to bury those who didn't take the flood seriously. Homes and businesses dry out, and streets are repaired. Bridges take a little longer.

Within a month, tourists are chuckling at the dry rivers and the signs that say, "Do Not Cross When Flooded."

And your average long-time Arizonan can't remember the last time it rained.

PRE-MONSOONAL SYNDROME

Use of "monsoon" to describe Arizona's summer precipitation has become so pervasive that Hubert F. Lauzon of Ash Fork asked his state senator to have the word outlawed. Natives like Lauzon and I prefer a word we have heard Hopi Indians use: "rain."

The word "monsoon" used to apply to the storms in the Indian Ocean, which change directions twice a year, and periodically flood the lowlands of Asia. Lately, it has come to describe any storm system with a counterclockwise motion, especially if it sucks up moisture from a cool ocean and drops it over warm land.

Some of Arizona's heaviest summer rains do come north from remnants of hurricanes and tropical storms. Before weathermen understood this, they called such a downpour a "Sonora storm" in honor of Arizona's neighbor to the south.

In *Climate of Phoenix,* master of wry understatement Robert J. Schmidli wrote: "The so-called 'Arizona Monsoon' is a marginal type monsoon, not nearly as intense as those in other places of the globe."

For statistical purposes, the Arizona monsoon exists any day when average dewpoints remain above 55. The average monsoon season is from July 7 to September 13.

Nowadays, TV and newspaper weather reporters set up a tedious monsoon watch in late June, as though they were sighting whales or waiting for an eclipse. It's a season I call PMS, for "pre-monsoonal syndrome."

—CHAPTER 9—

COLD FACTS, CHILLING FICTION

John Hance, who fancied the title "Captain," was the first promoter to build a trail into the Grand Canyon, and the first to advertise for tourists whom he could guide into the gorge.

Cap was famous for his stories. He told how he tried each year to predict the onset of winter, and move to the relative safety of Flagstaff. One winter night, when he was getting ready to leave, a terrible blizzard set in. Hance was snowbound in his cabin for a week, with no supplies except a jar of sorghum molasses and a box of soap. He said he'd heat molasses in the skillet, add soap flakes, and put in shavings from an old boot leg for flavoring.

Graham

"I tell you frankly," he said, "I have never liked the taste of soap from that day to this."

Many visitors don't realize that Arizona has forested mountains until they visit the Grand Canyon. Grand Canyon Village on the South Rim is at 6,826 feet elevation, and the North Rim Lodge 12 miles away is at 8,200 feet.

The cold facts out of Arizona's high mountain country almost rival Cap Hance's yarns. Hawley Lake in the White Mountains, half a state east-southeast of Grand Canyon, occasionally reports the coldest temperature in the United States, and holds the state's record for the lowest temperature, 40 degrees below zero.

Nearby Maverick, a logging town that existed only from 1948 to 1968, used to regularly be one of the coldest places in the nation. Its lowest reading was a mere minus-32. But the late Maverick still holds the state record for the coldest days in five months out of the year.

The mercury used to drop so abruptly in Maverick that it ripped off the brackets that held the thermometer to the Coca-Cola sign. One volunteer observer was quietly dismissed when weather officials found him digging a hole so the temperature would have more room to drop.

Arizona's cold facts amaze newcomers. I asked a young woman from New York, an intern in our office, if she knew the record snowfall for any one season in Arizona.

"Six inches?" she guessed.

"Nope. Four hundred inches."

She was so stunned that she couldn't think of anything to say. Come to think of it, she hasn't spoken to me since.

Getting Acquainted with Arizona's Other Extremes

My parents quit the desert in 1945 and started wintering in Camp Verde, still summering above the Mogollon Rim. The Verde Valley was a transition zone, as it turned out. It snowed now and then, but only a couple of inches. Then, in 1948, we moved to Flagstaff, 7,000 feet above sea level, a sawmill town and tourist hub in the world's largest ponderosa pine forest.

The winter that followed was one of the wetter ones on record. It snowed 22.2 inches late in December and the storm continued right on into January, 1949, when it snowed a record 104.8 inches during the month.

Flagstaff had modern snow removal equipment, but no place to dump the snow. At first, trucks dumped the plowed snow into canyons and arroyos around town, but the snow soon filled them. And then the truck drivers couldn't find a way to get their rigs above the head-high snow to dump them.

Flagstaff streets became tiny, narrow snow canyons, two lanes separated by a ridge of snow. I can still hear the rhythmic clink of tire chains, muffled by the snow. Only the hardiest individuals shoveled out their driveways.

We lived in a homemade trailer house on a flat lot east of Flagstaff. Snow soon drifted higher than the roof of the trailer. My brother and I had a great time that winter, because school was cancelled for several days, and he got a new sled for Christmas. Our mother does not remember it so fondly, for she had to deal with wet, smelly clothes, a wet, smelly dog, and tracked-in mud and ice. Although she has since retired to 4,700-foot Yarnell, which has an almost ideal climate, she still hates gloomy winter days.

That Flagstaff winter was some initiation to Arizona's other weather extreme, especially the morning we had to walk to the school bus stop when the temperature was 26 degrees below zero. The frozen ground rang like a steel deck beneath our feet. (The record at Flagstaff is 30 below, set back in 1937.)

The Santa Fe Railroad was still using steam engines in 1949. Steam from the whistle of a westbound freight froze and fell into a snowbank. Come the spring thaw, the notes were released on the air one morning. Every bull elk within earshot began to paw the ground, and

70

the stationmaster kept checking his watch to see if the Santa Fe had slipped an extra train in on him.

WILD WEST SCENARIOS

In 1874, the wagon train of mine and mill operator C.E. Hitchcock became snowbound in the mountains near Fort Verde, Arizona Territory. Lt. Calvin Duvall Cowles, 23, a handsome West Point graduate, led a rescue detail.

Daringly, Mrs. Hitchcock and her two daughters changed into the soldiers' spare trousers so they could ride to safety astride mules. The sight of 19-year-old Mary Hitchcock in trousers apparently beguiled Lt. Cowles. They were married two months later.

Then there's the story of Charles Henson Meadows, whose father and brother were killed in an Indian attack near Payson in 1882. Meadows traveled the world as "Arizona Charlie," a Wild West showman.

Meadows spent his last years at Yuma. When someone inquired about his health, he replied, "It'll be a snowy day in Yuma that they plant this old Hassayamper."

Arizona Charlie was buried December 12, 1932. That night it snowed a record 1.5 inches at Yuma.

The Mother of Arizona Winter Storms

But that wasn't the heaviest storm to hit the northern plateau country. The worst on record seems to be the one that clobbered most of northern Arizona in December, 1967. It was actually two storms, separated by one day, which somewhat complicated the official weather records. At Heber Ranger Station a few miles north of the Mogollon Rim, 67 inches fell in three days.

Official statistics go on and on. Unofficially, some local observers swore that the Rim, normally around 7,500 feet high, sank 17 5/8 inches under the weight of the snow.

"Seventeen and five-eighths inches?" an old-timer would say skeptically, shifting his tobacco to the other cheek.

"Seventeen and five-eighths inches," the weather observer would repeat, with a straight face. "Just about a cubit."

At Flagstaff, 83 inches of snow accumulated on the ground; Hawley Lake accumulated 102.7 inches. At Flagstaff and Grand Canyon, the temperature did not get above freezing for 10 consecutive days.

Life came to a standstill all across the Colorado Plateau. Traditionally, provisions are airlifted to the isolated Navajo Indians in the northeastern corner of the state during any heavy storm. In 1967, a lot of people and livestock south of the reservation stayed alive because of airlifts. A number of people died of exposure, or from heart attacks while shoveling snow from roofs that threatened to collapse. Many buildings collapsed despite human efforts.

I have been told that Indians still call that season "the year the White Mountains turned blue." One rural snowplow driver reported seeing eight tiny reindeer near McNary, but the sighting was never confirmed.

In the winter of 1972-73, Flagstaff received a record 210 inches of snow for the season, but it was spread out over several months, including one of the wettest Marches on record. That was the year Sunrise Mountain, a ski area in the White Mountains, received 123 inches of snow in March, and the record 400.90 inches for one season.

Arizonans remember these storms precisely because they are so exceptional. Flagstaff enjoys 79 percent of possible sunshine, exceeding the 73 percent for Miami,

Florida. The San Franciso Peaks, tallest in Arizona, rise behind the town, sometimes wearing a cap of snow to remind travelers that this is tall country.

IT'S A DRY SNOW

You have to have a sense of humor to live in a place called Snowflake, Arizona. So each Groundhog Day, citizens of Snowflake have a community breakfast featuring ground hog, i.e., sausage.

Weather had nothing to do with the naming of Snowflake. The town was named for Mormon pioneers Erastus Snow and William J. Flake. Being called a "flake" is not necessarilyan insult there-- many of the town's residents are named Flake. No two Flakes are alike.

Snowflake had 37 inches of snow once, but that was back in January, 1937, one of the coldest months in Arizona history. While the town gets mighty cold in winter, its average annual precipitation is only 11.35 inches. It is on the semi-arid Colorado Plateau; like Springerville and Winslow, its potential precipitation is robbed by mountains to the south and west.

On most days of the year, all highways and many secondary roads in the high country are open and clear. Mountain businessmen, who rely on visitors from Phoenix and Tucson for part of their income, become incensed when the big city news media make every storm sound like a blizzard. But enough stranded motorists have died in sudden winter storms that the flatland media dare not ignore it.

While southern Arizona doesn't get clobbered by so many big storms, it gets some snow. Steep mountains, taller than any in the eastern United States, rise abruptly from the desert floor. It's possible to climb 7,500 feet in perhaps 12 miles of lateral travel. So it's possible to get snowbound in the Chiricahuas, or to ski on Mount Lemmon near Tucson, while resorts below are filled with golfers and tennis players who came to Tucson to escape snow and get a winter tan. It even snows a bit now and then at Phoenix, Tucson and Yuma. Exact amounts can be found in The Old Newcomer's Almanac at the end of this volume.

"Sandshoes" Leave Long Tracks

Occasionally, I have used snowshoes to do my job as a reporter. Once, on a snow survey in the White Mountains, the government crew chief and I stepped off a snow cat without our snowshoes. I sank in snow up to my armpits. The crew chief was six inches shorter than I, and we were getting panicky by the time we retrieved him.

In eastern Quebec in 1982, I bought a pair of handmade snowshoes for my son, who was living in Flagstaff. The shoes were too large to fit into luggage or lockers. So I hand-carried them 3,000 miles on buses, trains and planes.

As I removed them from the overhead rack of a Canadian passenger train, I told a man from Toronto, "Mustn't forget my sand shoes."

"Oh, is that really what you use them for down there?"

He seemed so nice that I had to tell him the truth. But you should have seen the looks as I carried the snowshoes through the Phoenix airport terminal one night in late July.

Fog So Thick You Can Lie On It

Winter weather brings Arizona another phenomenon that you don't see in all those old John Wayne movies: fog.

74

Some years, an icy fog sets in along the valley of the Little Colorado River from St. Johns to Winslow, 110 miles away, and screws up travel in the region for weeks at a time. It also fills the valleys between the mesas farther north, on the Navajo Reservation, leaving the dark mesas like islands in a sea of cotton candy.

But one of the prettiest sights is when fog fills the Grand Canyon rim-to-rim, like a monstrous bowl of whipped cream. Cap Hance had fun with that one. Some evenings, he'd tell the dudes he was going to snowshoe across the canyon that night, after the fog froze. Watch for his campfire, he said. Any dude gullible enough to get up at 4 a.m. and look across the canyon would likely see the lights of an early tourist camp on the North Rim and think Hance had made it.

Or he might tell them he was going to ski across. "But the last time I tried it, I got about halfway across when the fog began to lift. I hurried around from one patch of fog to another, but I just couldn't make it. I finally hit a rock in the fog and wound up over there on top of Zoroaster Temple (a prominent butte in the Canyon)."

He was stranded there for four weeks, he said, before another fog filled the canyon. "It was a light fog," he said, "but by then, I was a lot lighter, too."

—CHAPTER 10—

THE BLASTED WINDS OF WINSLOW

Retired railroaders still talk about the day the wind died in Winslow. Older school teachers, whose numbers are dwindling, tell their pupils of that awesome event, caused by some mysterious atmospheric disturbance.

On that afternoon, a Little League play-off game was called because of calm. Citizens of the town, who habitually leaned into the wind, fell to the sidewalk when the wind suddenly died. Several were treated for minor injuries.

The terrifying silence convinced several hypochondriacs that they had gone deaf. (Many Winslowites actually have impaired hearing, because they keep their TV volume turned up so they can hear the weather forecast over the roar of the wind. See illustration facing page.)

Winslow is a railroad town on the Santa Fe's mainline across northern Arizona. It also is where Interstate 40, formerly U.S. Route 66, crosses the Little Colorado River. The corridor along U.S. 66 in northern Arizona used to be called "The Highline."

Winslow sits like a hairpiece on the nearly-bald pate of the Colorado Plateau. The wind seems to be working its way under the toupee, determined to blow the town away.

Other towns on The Highline claim to have mighty springtime winds: Kingman, Ash Fork, Holbrook. I can vouch for the fact that Flagstaff has some intolerable, persistent, icy spring winds. Far south of The Highline, at Springerville, spring winds drive all the barbs in a barbed wire fence down to the next fence post.

When I married, I took my bride from Springerville, her hometown, to Winslow, where I was editing a newspaper. She thoughtlessly opened an umbrella there one day, and was nearly dragged to death before I could catch her and throw her to the ground.

They Never Say, "Go Fly a Kite!"

Years later, I thought my memory was messing with my mind. The wind couldn't be as bad as I remembered. So I wrote a newspaper column about that wind. Those Winslow residents who could catch their newspapers that morning wrote to say I had grossly underestimated their beloved gale

Graham

One native, Margaret Heming, remembered a time the wind blew so fiercely that she and her aunt hid under a dining room table. After the wind died, Margaret went out into the street, where one wall of a department store had been blown down.

"People came out of stores and just looked at the damage in complete silence," she said.

George Spears wrote of a Winslow inventor who invented a kind of metal weather stripping to keep the red dust from blowing in around windows and doors.

"The only problem was that the darn strips would vibrate in any wind over 10 miles an hour. They would begin to hum, beelike, and as the wind speed increased, the pitch rose. On a good windy day these vibrations rising and falling with variations in the wind speed reminded you of 40 Mormon Tabernacle Choirs warming up for *Battle Hymn of the Republic*."

I checked weather records and found relatively modest peak gusts as high as 63 miles an hour, although gusts of 40 miles per hour occur in every month of the year. But the "mean" prevailing winds are higher than those in other towns.

I had heard that Winslow had the only weather station in Arizona where the rain gauge is installed horizontally, rather than vertically. The National Weather Service denied that.

My friend Vada Carlson wrote a folksy history of Winslow, *A Town Is Born*. Nearly everyone she interviewed talked about the wind. Vada said, "It was usually there, snatching hats, immodestly lifting skirts, ruining complexions, messing hair."

One man who worked outdoors remembered the wind fondly because it cooled him in the afternoon sun.

"Of course, it did get pretty rough off and on. Blew the shingles off my house one day. Peppered us with gravel now and then, so we had to stop work and close our eyes.

"But by and large, I guess I'd say we'd rather have the wind than the quiet. At night, in summer, it blew mosquitoes away so's we could sit outside without being eaten alive, and most of the time we just bent into it and went our way, in spite of it. You took it for granted, like a trademark."

In 1978, I presided over a statewide liar's contest for the Sunday magazine of *The Arizona Republic*. Jean Black, a Winslow home economist, submitted the winning entry, which included these observations on Winslow:

"Stopped trains have the wheels chocked.

"It is believed the Tower of Pisa was built by a contractor who had lived here too long.

"The residents don't need to have a dentist clean their teeth--they just smile during a sandstorm and the tartar is blasted right off."

Black told about the chamber of commerce manager, new to town, who thought it would be fun to hold a kite-flying contest. But all the little contestants suffered rope burns, and some of the larger kits were later intercepted by the Royal Canadian Air Force.

The Winslow airport had special problems: "One pilot neglected to use full throttle during landing and was blown backwards off the runway. Another complained that he used more fuel taxiing to the terminal than he did flying from Seattle."

Helicopter pilots who overnight at Winslow Airport are cautioned to remove their rotors. One thought he could simply chain down the rotor; next morning, he found the pilotless craft hovering at 500 feet. Seventeen days later, two cowboys roped it and pulled it down.

During one particularly windy day, Black wrote, a Santa Fe train consisting of 97 empty cars was blown over. Operating rules were changed so that (1) empties are alternated with loaded cars or (2) deadheading train crews are used as ballast.

Black concluded: "If you decide to investigate all this yourself, you can't miss Winslow on I-40. As you leave the town, you see highway signs reading: 'CAUTION, CALM AIR'."

CHALLENGING WINSLOW'S SUPREMACY

Marshall Trimble wanted to be a professional baseball player. When that didn't work out, he became Arizona's best-known pop historian and folklore dealer. In a letter to the author, Trimble claimed wind supremacy for Ash Fork:

"Winslow's wind was slow compared with my hometown of Ash Fork, where it started blowing around January 1 each year and didn't quit until sometime around midnight on December 31. But it was at its worst in the spring.

"I was the catcher on my old high school baseball team and had to learn to gauge my throws to second base. If the wind was blowing from left, I threw to third and let it blow into second. When los vientos came from right, I just reversed things and rifled the ball to first. That old baseball hit second base right on the money every time.

"I was a pretty good catcher in northern Arizona, but when I came south and played for Phoenix College in 1958, the coach benched me for always throwing to the wrong base. A scout from Chicago was interested in signing me. He said I'd fit right in. But after playing in northern Arizona, I figured any other windy place would have been a step down."

Arizona's Portable Real Estate

South of the Mogollon Rim, the winds are rarely violent. Phoenix, Tucson and Yuma usually benefit from gentle breezes. Driving U.S. 93 in the calm of June, you could believe the old gag about the rancher who had to take down one of his windmills because there wasn't enough wind for two.

However, you need to be aware of some violent winds that can occur in desert country, usually in summer.

The whirlwind called a "dust devil" is kind of cute, a little funnel of western Americana spinning along the desert, going with the prevailing breeze, bending and skipping and waltzing to follow the terrain. The vortex begins on a hot summer day, and picks up dust and debris which helps define its shape. Most dust devils are only a few feet across and maybe 100 feet tall.

Sometimes, however, dust devils grow up to be towering, menacing funnel clouds. Periodically, one will damage houses, or demolish mobile homes, or cause an automobile accident. Dust devils can act like tornadoes, except that a tornado dips down from the clouds.

There have been a good many damaging tornadoes in Arizona over the past century. However, unless a qualified observer is on hand, the National Weather Service is reluctant to name a funnel cloud a tornado; the NWS prefers to believe in dust devils. Therefore, an Arizonan who finds his home unroofed or the aluminum skin peeled from his mobile home is likely to also witness a jurisdictional squabble dispute between those who believe it was a tornado, and those who insist it was only a dust devil.

The most menacing summer wind, and the most irritating, is that which causes the dust storm, or the sand storm. Just before towering cumulonimbus clouds release their lightning and rain, they create a wall of wind below and ahead of them.

This wind sucks up dirt and creates what from a distance seems to be a large curtain of brown velvet moving regally across the horizon. This awe-inspiring sight is one that ought not to be missed, but is best viewed from a distance.

"My God, what is that?" a dude asked one day when a brown curtain loomed over the Gila.

A native replied with a straight face, "The river's up."

A dust storm marches relentlessly across the open desert. When it encounters an interstate highway, such as the one between Tucson and Phoenix, it may cause terrible chain collisions of automobiles and trucks. (Seriously, if you are caught in such a storm, the Arizona Highway Patrol advises you to pull off the highway as far as possible--and turn off your lights so that an 18-wheeler doesn't try to follow you.)

Then it storms into the Phoenix metropolitan area, which has an abnormal number of residential swimming pools, all of which will have to be cleaned again the following day. With luck, the dust storm is followed by drenching thundershowers. But too frequently, the rain amounts to only a few drops, enough to encrust automobile windshields with mud spots.

A Not-so-Mellow Drama of Arizona Weather

Let's return for a moment to July, 1910. Newspapers in that era had a marvelous sense of melodrama, and in a few days they capsuled the essence of summer weather in the desert. First, Chauncey Rhodes, a traveling salesman from Philadelphia, set out on horseback to visit his sister at Hillside, 100 miles northwest of Phoenix. He got lost and would have died of thirst, had not a sudden thunderstorm drenched him and created pools of water.

A similar storm in the Phoenix area broke the banks of the Arizona Canal, flooding farms along Indian Bend Wash. That rain was preceded by a series of dust storms, one of which almost claimed the life of Paradise Valley homesteader L.M. Fitzhugh. A newspaper reported:

"Like a great black curtain the sandstorm swept on, and as it drew nearer, Fitzhugh, fearing that his horse, which was tied about thirty feet away, would take fright at it, went over to the horse and took the bridle.

"When the sandstorm struck with the force of a cyclone, he caught hold of the tree to which the horse was tied to keep from being blown from his feet. Gravel as large as a hazelnut struck him in the face and rattled against the cabin like hail.

"The atmosphere was so nearly a solid mass of dirt that breathing was impossible. Fitzhugh fell to the ground and placed his handkerchief over his face. He held his breath, for breathing into the floating dirt was as impossible as breathing under water. He felt strangulation clutching at his throat and knew that he could endure it for but a few seconds longer. When he could get his breath no longer he thought to get over it as quickly as possible. He drew in a breath of the swimming sand. He might as well have tried to breathe in a sand pile. He sprang to his feet, thinking to run for the house, but was blown down instantly and at the same moment the storm passed."

—CHAPTER 11—

FIRST AND LAST RESORT

Dick Wick Hall assigned to himself, and to all of Salome's other characters, a professional ignorance of the genteel, eastern game called golf.

"We can't figure out," Hall wrote, "whether a score of 72 means that he made it around in 72 hours or 72 days or used up 72 balls going around."

Hall invented the Greasewood Lynx Golf Course, 23 miles long, and made it famous through stories in *The Saturday Evening Post.* A water wagon followed players around the course. One spring Hall wrote that ranchers were angry because they couldn't hire help; the cowboys had all gone to work as mounted caddies.

Writer-artist Ross Santee came along a few years later with his book about the family that created the Bar X Golf Course as a new source of revenue for a profitless ranch. Santee wrote that the No. 2 hole was 15 miles long, and no dude would be allowed to start without a full canteen. "Where Black Canyon cuts in about 15 miles up is what really makes it sporty. By carrying the canyon on this shot, a dude can cut off at least two miles."

Fact: Cowboys were playing their own variations of golf from horseback, before 1900.

Fact: Hall actually built a rudimentary nine-hole golf course at Salome, and today his greatest windy seems to have been prophetic--there are more than 200 golf courses in Arizona.

Many of the better known courses are attached to winter resorts, places far more pretentious than Hall's Salome. Others are retirement communities. It is not by accident that some of America's most successfull retirement communities are named Sun City, Sun City West and Sun Lakes.

The possibilities of the winter resort trade occurred early to Arizona promoters. Before the turn of the century, the Pilot Knob Hotel in Yuma wore a big sign across its front: "Free board every day that the sun doesn't shine." That's a pretty safe offer in a town where the sun shines 91 percent of the possible hours in a year.

For a long time, sufferers of asthma and tuberculosis, with or without money came to Arizona to get well in the sun.

Graham

Oracle Was Cool in the Summer

Bill and Ann Neal created the best of both worlds. Neal, son of a black father and Cherokee mother, had become a prosperous Tucson freighter. In 1895, the Neals opened Mountain View Hotel at Oracle, near 4,500 feet elevation on the northern slopes of the Santa Catalina Mountains. Guests rode there on Neals' stagecoach line.

The Mountain View attracted not only sun-seekers and health-seekers from the East in winter, but Tucson residents who wanted to cool off in the summer. One frequent guest was William F. "Buffalo Bill" Cody, who had ridden with Neal when they were Army scouts on the Great Plains.

And it also was in 1895 that that the ritzy Castle Hot Springs resort hotel north of Phoenix began to attract monied people to relax in the sun and the mineral spa. After a long train ride, guests rode stagecoaches 28 miles over rough desert, which gave the resort a magnificent isolation from the troubles of the world.

A few years later, Phoenix canal builder and land developer W.J. Murphy needed a lodge where he could entertain prospective investors. So he built Ingleside a few miles northeast of Phoenix. Its attractions included a rudimentary golf course featuring oiled sand in lieu of grass.

Murphy and his son Ralph also developed some secluded homes at Ingleside, attractive to winter visitors who could afford to follow the sun. One early winter resident was Thomas R. Marshall, vice-president of the United States under Woodrow Wilson and the man who said, "What the country needs is a good five-cent cigar."

About 1921, Ralph Murphy turned Ingleside into the Phoenix area's first winter resort, a semi-rustic place where businessmen from Chicago could relax in the winter sun. In the same era, the Arizona Inn was built in Tucson by Isabella Greenway, who would become

Arizona's first (and so far only) women U.S. representative.

Resorts blossomed after that: Jokake Inn and the Arizona Biltmore near Phoenix, the San Marcos in Chandler, El Conquistador in Tucson, the Wigwam at Litchfield Park.

Where the Southern Pacific and Sante Fe had earlier advertised excursion fares to carry Arizonans to the California coast in summer, they began to advertise nationally to bring visitors to Phoenix and Tucson in the winter.

Architect Frank Loyd Wright was an early visitor to Jokake and the Biltmore. Later he established a winter studio and school near Scottsdale, initiating a large body of folklore about which Arizona buildings were or were not designed by Wright.

Scottsdale started in the 1880s as a citrus development, and remained a dusty crossroads until after World War II. Then it blossomed as the center of the resort industry in central Arizona, a glitzy place that called itself, ironically, "The Wests Most Western Town."

Irving Berlin stayed at the Biltmore in November, 1937, while he was writing the music for the movie *Alexander's Ragtime Band* and *Carefree*. "Sunshine is why I'm here now, " Berlin said lyrically. "I particularly like the quality of the Arizona sunshine."

Publisher Henry Luce and Ambassador Clare Booth Luce enjoyed their winter visits so well they became residents. So did Erma Bombeck, Hugh Downs and dozens of other notables.

Arizona Was the Last Chance For "Lungers"

The finer resorts learned early that it did not help their images when they attracted asthmatics and tuberculars, even those who had money. So the hotels advertised pointedly that they were not sanatoriums.

But the health-seekers came anyway with or without money. For many, the dry climate of Arizona was their last resort. They established communities of tents and shacks. One of these, Sunnyslope, is now a respectable area of Phoenix. Another nearby "lunger" community, Cactus, lost its identity as it was swallowed by the expanding city.

Many lungers got well and became prominent Arizonans, or at least healthy ones. (Assuming that they did not succumb to other climate-related aliments. Arizona has one of the highest skin cancer rates in the country, and many allergies are aggravated by airborn pollen, dust and other sinister missles carried on the desert breeze.)

Operators of "dude ranches" wrote another chapter of this story from the 1920s into the 1940s. People of means loved to come to the desert and play cowboy, with help from real cowboys. Wickenberg called itself "The Dude Ranch Capitol of the World," and Tucson was not far behind.

Today's guests at the Boulders near Phoenix or Loew's Ventana canyon ranch near Tucson are more likely to be playing tennis than playing John Wayne, jogging instead of riding horseback.

Bird-watching in the Winter Sun

As soon as railroads crossed Arizona in the 1870s and 1880s, tramps and drifters began to take advantage of Arizona' winter climate. These visitors were called "snowbirds." For better or worse the term has been applied to a much more responsible class of visitors.

Businessmen call the mobile visitors "winter visitors," out of deference to the substantial amount of money they spend in Arizona. Let's not kill the snowgoose that lays the golden egg. But inevitably, they are know to others as "snowbirds." If you are such a winter visitor, forgive us.

They flock to Mesa and Apache Junction east of Phoenix, to Tucson, and to the desert towns of western Arizona. Many are farmers and retirees from the northern United States. Others are farmers from western Canada, who spend the winter in Arizona seeking their national identity. In my own travels I have met several Canadians who know Mesa better than I do.

Yuma's population swells in winter with thousands of regular winter visitors. I heard two Midwesterners, who met at Yuma each winter, jawing at each other in mock exasperation.

"I'm going to spend next winter in Mesa," one threatened, "so I won't have to put up with you."

"No you won't," his friend said. "They'd run right over you up there."

Inevitably, there is a conflict between the purposeful driving of locals in the Mesa area and the slow, indecisive driving of the winter visitors. A working Arizonan has to keep his speed up to get anywhere in the sprawling cities of the Salt River Valley, but he frequently gets trapped behind a motorhome with North Dakota plates, or a meandering Lincoln Continental from Alberta. A farmer from Saskatchewan, accustomed to two-lane farm roads, takes full advantage of the multiple-lane boulevards in Mesa and Apache Junction, wandering freely from lane to lane.

The population of tiny Quartzsite is said to reach 100,000 in February, when suburbs of recreational vehicles sprawl across the desert. Nearby Salome draws visitors who seek a quieter lifestyle. An old rancher from Montana told me that coming to Salome each winter was like a reunion, and not always a happy one: "Every year, a few more old friends don't make it down here, and you wonder if they died during the winter."

How Far is it to That Purple Mountain

Visitors learn to appreciate the desert in ways that natives may not. And they learn quickly of one climate-related phenomenon that needs to be explored here.

With little mist in the clear, dry air, geographic features like mountains look closer than they actually are. This was first reported by Spanish soldiers who visited the Grand Canyon in 1540. They didn't believe it was as far to that little ribbon of Colorado River below as the Indians said it was. More athletic soldiers spent half a day climbing one-third of the way down, and decided the Indians were telling the truth.

The illusion has amazed newcomers ever since--and killed a few, who got lost on the way to distant mountains that looked so near.

In Wickenberg, they tell about the guest who left a dude ranch one morning to walk to an inviting mountain. Cowboys who rescued him at sunset found he had made it only half way there, and he was dehydrated out of his mind.

A couple of days later, the dude wranglers found the same man undressing beside a tiny creek, a trickle of water maybe 18 inches across.

"Why are yore taking off your clothes?" a wrangler asked.

"I'm going to swim this river."

—CHAPTER 12—

THE OLD NEWCOMER'S ALMANAC

Highest point in Arizona: Mt. Humphreys, one of the San Francisco Peaks north of Flagstaff, 12,643 feet.

Second-highest point in Arizona: Mt. Baldy in the White Mountains, 11,590 feet.

Lowest point in Arizona: About 75 feet where the Colorado River flows into Mexico south of Yuma.

Elevation at Phoenix: 1,100 feet.

Elevation at Tucson: 2,400 feet.

Lowest communities in Arizona: Gadsden, 95 feet; Somerton, 101 feet; Yuma, 141 feet.

Highest communities in Arizona: Alpine and Summerhaven, 8,000 feet.

HIGHEST OFFICIAL TEMPERATURE READINGS

Arizona:	127	Fort Mohave, June 15, 1986, and Parker July 7, 1905
Phoenix:	122	June 26, 1990
Tucson:	117	June 26, 1990
Yuma:	123	September 1, 1950
Flagstaff:	97	July 5, 1973
Winslow:	109	July 13, 1971
United States:	134	July 10, 1913, at Death Valley, California

LOWEST OFFICIAL TEMPERATURE READINGS

Arizona	-40	Hawley Lake, January 7, 1971
Phoenix	16	January 7, 1913
Tucson	16	December 24, 1974
Yuma	24	January 8, 1971
Flagstaff	-30	January 22, 1937
Winslow	-18	January 22, 1937
United States	-80	Prospect Creek, Alaska January 23,1971
Lower 48 States	-70	Rogers Pass, Montana, January 20, 1954

LOCATION OF RECORD HIGH TEMPERATURES FOR EACH MONTH

January: 93, Maricopa, 1912; **February:** 97, Yuma and Casa Grande, 1986; **March:** 102, Parker, 1930; **April:** 111, Santa Rosa, 1962; **May:** 120, Mohawk, Yuma and Casa Grande, 1910; **June:** 127, Fort Mohave, 1896; **July:** 127, Parker, 1905; **August:** 126, Parker, 1905; **September:** 122, Mohawk and Ehrenberg, 1950; **October:** 114, Gila Bend, 1980; **November:** 100, Mohawk, 1918; Parker, 1915; Granite Reef Dam, 1931; **December:** 92, Parker, 1901; Bouse, 1958; Mesa, 1964.

RECORD LOW TEMPERATURES FOR EACH MONTH

January: -40, Hawley Lake, 1971; **February:** -32, Maverick, 1965; **March:** -26, Maverick, 1966; **April:** -16 Hawley Lake, 1980; **May:** 5, Maverick, 1950; **June:** 13, Maverick, 1954; **July:** 25, Maverick, 1962; Flagstaff, 1987; **August:** 24, Flagstaff, 1968; **September:** 12, Sunset Crater, 1978; **October:** -5, Sunrise Mountain, 1972; **November:** -21, St. Johns, 1931; Clay Springs, 1976; **December:** -30, Fort Valley, 1978.

AVERAGE ANNUAL PRECIPITATION

Phoenix	7.11 inches
Tucson	11.14 inches
Yuma	2.65 inches
Flagstaff	20.86 inches
Winslow	7.64 inches

RAIN STOPS AT THE CATTLE GUARD

To hear an Arizona farmer or rancher tell it, the rain always stops at his fence line. I have, in fact, seen a heavy New Mexico thundershower stop at the Arizona border. I wouldn't be surprised to see a storm quit at the meandering boundary between Scottsdale and Phoenix.

It is believed to have been famed cowboy writer-artist Ross Santee who wrote in an anonymous 1939 federal guidebook, "Desert rains are usually so definitely demarked that the story of the man who washed his hands in the edge of an Arizona thundershower without wetting his cuffs seems almost credible."

One northern Arizona cattleman asked this blessing during a drought: "Thanks, Lord, for the food that we are about to eat. Lord, I ain't asked you for much since the time my daughter run off with a forest ranger, but we sure could use a rain. And Lord, if you can't make it rain on my place, please don't let it rain on Babbitts or Wingfields."

GREATEST PRECIPITATION IN ONE HOUR
Arizona 3.25 inches
Tempe Citrus Experiment Station, September 14, 1969

| Phoenix | 1.72 inches, August 18, 1966 |
| United States | 12 inches, Holt, Missouri, June 22, 1947 and Kilauea Sugar Plantation, Hawaii, January 24-25, 1956 |

GREATEST PRECIPITATION IN 24 HOURS

Arizona	11.40 inches, Workman Creek (30 miles north-northwest of Globe) September 4-5, 1970
Phoenix	4.98 inches July 1-2, 1911.
United States	43 inches Alvin, Texas July 25-26, 1979

GREATEST PRECIPITATION IN ONE YEAR

Arizona	58.92 inches, Hawley Lake, 1978
Phoenix	19.73 inches, 1905
United States	704.83 inches, Kukui, Hawaii, 1982

LEAST PRECIPITATION IN ONE CALENDAR YEAR

Arizona	0.07 inch, Davis Dam, 1956
Phoenix	2.82 inches, 1956
United States	0.0 inches, Death Valley, California, 1929, and Bagdad, California, 1913

GOOD DAYS FOR OUTDOOR WEDDINGS

In the first 95 years of weather records for Phoenix (1896-1990), there has never been measurable precipitation on four days of the year: May 23 and 25, and June 5 and 11.

ODD FACTS ABOUT ARIZONA'S PHENOMENAL SNOWSTORMS

Note: In each of the several time frames in which snow amounts are measured, the record for Phoenix is 1 inch, the amount measured January 20, 1933, and January 20-21, 1937. Unofficially, the 1937 blizzard dropped as much as 4 inches in some parts of the city. Snowfall of less than 1 inch has been recorded several times over 95 years of record-keeping.

Greatest snowfall in one storm:

Arizona	67 inches Heber Ranger Station, December 13-16,1967
Tucson	6.8 inches December 8, 1971
Yuma	1.5 inches December 12-13, 1932
United States	189 inches Mt. Shasta Ski Bowl, California, February 13-19, 1959

In one calendar month:

Arizona	123 inches Sunrise Mountain March, 1973
Flagstaff	104.8 inches, January, 1949
Winslow	39.6 inches, December, 1967
United States	390 inches Tamarack, California January, 1911

Greatest snow depth:

Arizona	91 inches Hawley Lake December 21, 1967
Tucson	6.8 inches, December 8, 1971
Flagstaff	83 inches, December 19-20, 1967
United States	451 inches Tamarack, California March 11, 1911

Greatest snowfall in one season:
  Arizona   400.9 inches
                   Sunrise Mountain
                   1972-73
  Flagstaff   210 inches, 1972-73
  United States   1122 inches
                   Rainier Paradise Ranger Station,
                   Washington, 1971-72

THE COLDEST MONTH

Climate of Arizona says January, 1937, was "probably the coldest month on record in Arizona. Statewide, the temperatures measured 10.7 degrees below normal." Flagstaff's average temperature that month was 12.6 degrees. On January 22, the low temperature there was -30, a record for the station.

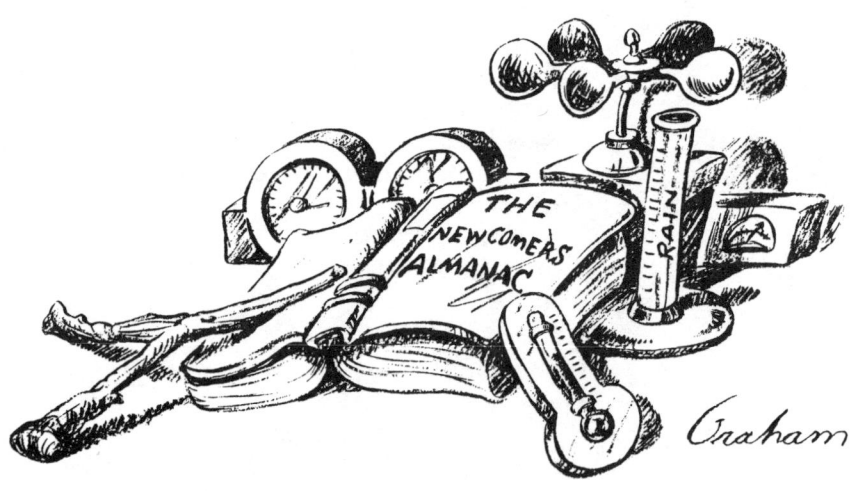

HIGHEST WIND VELOCITY, PEAK GUST

Arizona   92 miles per hour
                 Mesa
                 August 13, 1983
Phoenix   86 miles per hour, July 7, 1976
United States   231 miles per hour
                 Mt. Washington, New Hampshire,
                 April 12, 1934

UNOFFICIAL RECORDS

Climatologists acknowledge that it may have been hotter or colder or wetter in Arizona than official records indicate. But they are understandably cautious about how and where "official" measurements are recorded.

Experts acknowledge some "unofficial" records, as though they would like to believe them. For instance, the 5.10 inches of rain that fell on Tucson the afternoon of July 11, 1878, is the "unofficial" record for any two-hour period in Arizona history.

Weathermen lament the bad luck of the official observer at Fort Mohave in August, 1898: "On the 28th, we had the biggest rain in 10 or 15 years, and to my regret, between the rain and the furious wind, my rain gauge was upset. To give an idea of the amount of rain that fell, and which lasted only 45 minutes, I had a wash tub set out on the mesa, clear of everything, and the water after the rain, measured 8 inches."

Another observer estimated that 8 inches of rain fell at Crown King in one hour and 15 minutes August 6, 1948. A severe storm damaged mines near the Bradshaw Mountains town, and isolated its residents for three days.

GREATEST DAILY TEMPERATURE RANGE

Phoenix

48 degrees (59 minimum, 107 maximum), June 13, 1917; and again (48 minimum, 96 maximum) April 17, 1919

Arizona

71 degrees, Hawley Lake, February 2, 1973 (-18 minimum, 53 maximum)

Arizona Statewide

89 degrees on October 16, 1973, when the minimum temperature at Alpine was 16, the maximum at Gila Bend 105; and February 23, 1974, with a morning low of -7 at Hawley Lake and an afternoon high of 82 at Gila Bend

U.S. (lower 48 states)

158 degrees January 20, 1954, when the low was -70 at Rogers Pass, Montana, and the high was 88 at 40-mile Bend, Florida

AVERAGE "NORMAL" MAXIMUM TEMPERATURES AT PHOENIX

Based on a 1961-1990 average

June	July	August
103.4	105.8	103.6

December	January	February
66.3	66.0	70.8

MILESTONE DATES IN PHOENIX IN SUMMER

"Average" dates, based on 95-year records (1896-1990) and the latest 30-year records (1961-1990), suggest Phoenix temperatures have been increasing--at least in the "heat island" at Sky Harbor International Airport, where official readings are taken.

First 100-degree day:
   95 years   May 15
   30 years   May 6
   Earliest ever: March 26, 1988
Last 100-degree day:
   95 years   September 27
   30 years   September 28
   Latest ever: October 20, 1921
First 110-degree day:
   95 years   June 19
   30 years   June 14
   Earliest ever: May 8, 1989
Last 110-degree day:
   95 years   August 7
   30 years   August 18
   Latest ever   September 12, 1971
Onset of the "monsoon" season:
   Average date   July 7
   Earliest date   June 16, 1925
   Latest date   July 25, 1987
End of the monsoon season:
   Average date   September 13
   Earliest date   September 1, 1948
   Latest date   October 10, 1977, 1983

NOTABLE DRY SPELLS

Droughts have been too numerous to mention here. However, a few dry spells stand out. The longest Phoenix has gone without measurable rain was 160 days, from December 30, 1971, to June 6, 1972.

From September 12 to November 18, 1898, there was no measurable rain anywhere in Arizona Territory.

Since record-keeping began, there have been only six calendar months during which no "measurable" precipitation (more than a trace) fell anywhere in Arizona—November, 1894, and November, 1903. The most recent rainless month was November, 1917.

INDEX

U
Unofficial records - 72, 97

V
Verde Valley - 69, 70

W
Washington School - 45, 46
White Mountains - 27, 69,
72, 74
Wickenburg - 60, 88, 90
Wigwam Resort - 87
Wikle, John - 17, 43
Winslow - 76-79, 93
Wood, Richard A. - 64, 87
Wright, Frank Lloyd - 87

Y
Yuma - 15, 53, 89, 92-93
   average rainfall - 60
   sunshine - 2, 85